Teaching Entrepreneurship

Peter van der Sijde • Annemarie Ridder
Gerben Blaauw • Christoph Diensberg
Editors

Teaching Entrepreneurship

Cases for Education and Training

Publication was done within the project activities of BEPART – Baltic Entrepreneurship Partners, part-financed by the European Union, Programme Interreg III C. All information herein reflects the authors' view only; the EU and related organizations are not liable for any use that may be made of the information.

Physica-Verlag

A Springer Company

Dr. Peter van der Sijde
Annemarie Ridder, MSc.
Dr. Gerben Blaauw
University of Twente
Dutch Institute for Knowledge
Intensive Entrepreneurship
Capitool 15
7521 PL Enschede
Netherlands

Christoph Diensberg
Universität Rostock
Fak. Wirtschafts- u.
Sozialwissenschaft
Lehrst. für Konjunktur und
Wachstum
Ulmenstr. 69
18057 Rostock
Germany

ISBN: 978-3-7908-2037-9   e-ISBN: 978-3-7908-2038-6

Library of Congress Control Number: 2008930150

Cover design: WMX Design, Heidelberg

9 8 7 6 5 4 3 2 1

springer.com

Contents

Contributors

J. Andrijevskaja
Centre for Entrepreneurship, Faculty of Economics and Business Administration,
University of Tartu, Tartu, Estonia

C. Diensberg
HIE-RO, University of Rostock, Rostock, Germany

P. Dreisler
Aarhus School of Business, University of Aarhus, Aarhus, Denmark

H. Hannula
HAMK University of Applied Sciences, Hämeenlinna, Finland

T. Kauppi
University of Tampere, Tampere, Finland

J. Klich
Jagiellonian University, Kraków, Poland

P. Kyrö
University of Tampere, Tampere, Finland
and
Helsinki School of Economics, Helsinki, Finland

P. Malinen
Kajaani University of Applied Sciences, Kajaani, Finland

T. Mets
Centre for Entrepreneurship, Faculty of Economics and Business Administration,
University of Tartu, Tartu, Estonia

P. Milius
KTU regional Science Park, Kaunas, Lithuania

M. Niemi
Helsinki School of Economics, Helsinki, Finland

M. Nurminen
University of Tampere, Tampere, Finland

S. Pajari-Stylman
HAMK University of Applied Sciences, Hämeenlinna, Finland

P. Partanen
Kajaani University of Applied Sciences, Kajaani, Finland

A. Ridder
University of Twente, Enschede, The Netherlands

J. Rosiński
Jagiellonian University, Kraków, Poland

J. Sarkiene
KTU regional Science Park, Kaunas, Lithuania

P. van der Sijde
University of Twente, Enschede, The Netherlands

U. Venesaar
Tallinn School of Economics and Business Administration, Tallinn, Estonia

Teaching Entrepreneurship: An Introduction

"Entrepreneurship that is something you learn in practice". "Entrepreneurship is learning by doing". This is often heard when you tell others that you teach entrepreneurship, but maybe entrepreneurship is more "doing by learning". Nevertheless, in entrepreneurship practice and theory are interwoven. For this reason the Learning Cycle introduced by Kolb (1984) is an often used teaching approach.

According to this Learning Cycle there are four phases ("cycle") that are connected:

1. Concrete experience ("doing", "experiencing")
2. Reflection ("reflecting on the experience")
3. Conceptualization ("learning from the experience")
4. Experimentation ("bring what you learned into practice")

In teaching you can enter this cycle at any stage, depending on the students. And that brings us to the different types of students. Based on Hills et al. (1998) a plethora of student groups can be distinguished (of course this list is not exhaustive), e.g:

- Ph.D. students, who do a doctoral programme in Entrepreneurship; the emphasis is on theory/science.
- DBA students, who do a doctoral programme that is, in comparison to the Ph.D. more practice oriented.
- MBA students, who take entrepreneurship as one of the courses in their programme. Most of the time MBA students are mature students, who after some work experience return to the university; the programme is practice oriented.
- M.Sc. students, who do a Master programme in Entrepreneurship or take entrepreneurship courses in their Business Administration programme, and follow a more scientifically oriented programme; most of the time the students do not have relevant work experience.
- Bachelor students. There are different options for Bachelor students in universities:

- – Introductory course in Entrepreneurship for all students.
- – Elective Minor programme in Entrepreneurship for all students.
- – Bachelor programme in Entrepreneurship or with a focus on Entrepreneurship.
- • Extracurricular courses for interested students.
- • Entrepreneurs and also here different groups can be distinguished, e.g.
  - – Student-entrepreneurs: students who have a registered company (e.g. with the Chamber of Commerce, or have a VAT number).
  - – Graduate entrepreneurs: students who just finished their studies and start a company.
  - – Experienced entrepreneurs: entrepreneurs with some years of experience.

Returning to Kolb's Learning Cycle it means that for entrepreneurship teaching there is no "one size that fits all", a course or a programme should be designed for a target group. This brings us to two related topics: the learning outcomes and the different approaches ("concepts") to entrepreneurship in relation to the target groups.

It is obvious that entrepreneurship programmes for entrepreneurs have different learning outcomes compared to those for students. For example, entrepreneurs want to learn how to write a convincing business plan, while (some) students have to pass their examinations or have their paper accepted by the teaching staff. Some students want to learn and increase their skills (and competencies). Over the year many different approaches to entrepreneurship haven been proposed; e.g.

> *Entrepreneurship = Process of realizing opportunities*
> *Entrepreneurship = Set of competencies*

In the first approach entrepreneurship is seen as a process of realizing opportunities and it is rooted in the literature on "opportunity recognition" (see e.g. Davidsson 2004; Van der Veen and Wakkee 2004). The focus is on the process and the entrepreneur is part of this process. Examples of teaching and curricula can be found in the chapters by Dreisler, Venesaar, Milius & Sarkiene, Kyrö & Niemi and Van der Sijde & Ridder. The teaching focuses on the process of bringing opportunities to market. The learning outcome is, on a theoretical level, an understanding of the process and its resources; on the practical level, the elaboration of the resources in a business case or a business plan.

The second approach is a practical approach to entrepreneurship as a set of competencies (e.g. Gibb 1997; Hannon 2006). The focus is on the competencies of the entrepreneurs who drive the entrepreneurial process. Examples of teaching and curricula can be found in the chapters by Diensberg, Hannula & Pajari-Stylman, Malinen & Partanen, Andrijevskaja & Mets and Rosiński & Klich. This determines what is being taught and the focus is on the extension of the behavioural repertoire of the entrepreneur (as learning outcomes).

Two other approaches worth mentioning are:

> *Entrepreneurship = Starting a company*
> *Entrepreneurship = Management of a small company*

The third approach is, again, a practical approach that focuses on entrepreneurship as starting a company. Such courses are mostly about writing a business plan for presentation to financiers: target-oriented. Such an approach is very suitable for (starting) entrepreneurs who seek finance for their venture. A fourth approach is entrepreneurship as management of a small company – an approach often used in MBA curricula for post-experiential students. The emphasis is on managing the processes in a young company. Of course these are only four approaches and probably there are others still.

Finally, also the context of teaching is important and this context varies. There always is the "old-fashioned" classroom teaching (groups of students) to individual coaching, but there are also the other learning environments varying from the concrete (a "venture" environment, "real life" environment) to the virtual (a "virtual" community) – see Final Chapter by Kyrö, Kauppi & Nurminen.

This book is the result of a project – BEPART (Baltic Entrepreneurship Partners) and was co-financed by the EU Programme Interreg III C". It addresses different aspects of learning environments, target groups and approaches to teaching entrepreneurship in the cases of the universities.

References

Davidsson P (2004) Researching Entrepreneurship. Boston: Springer

Gibb A (1997) Small Firms' Training and Competitiveness. Building upon the small business as a learning organisation. International Small Business Journal, 14, 13–29

Hills GE & Morris MH (1998) Entrepreneurship Education: A conceptual model and review. In M.G. Scott, P. Rosa & H. Klandt (eds.) Educating Entrepreneurs for Wealth Creation. Aldershot: Ashgate publishing (p. 38–58)

Hannon P (2006) Enterprise and Entrepreneurship in English Higher Education. Birmingham: NCGE

Kolb DA (1984) Experiential Learning: Experience as the source of learning and development. Englewood Cliffs: Prentice Hall

Van der Veen M & Wakkee I (2004) Understanding the Entrepreneurial Process. In: D. Watkins (ed.), ARPENT-Annual Review of Progress in Entrepreneurship, Volume 2. Brussels: EFMD

Entrepreneurship: From Opportunity to Action: The Entrepreneurial Process

P. Dreisler

Aarhus School of Business, University of Aarhus, Aarhus, Denmark

An Inter-Institutional Cooperation

In 1989 an informal cooperation was initiated between teachers from three HE institutions in Aarhus – the engineering college, the school of architecture's institute of industrial design, and the business school, ASB. The teachers decided to set up mixed project groups for their students to carry out projects in what was then called "product development". The cooperation was initiated quite informally and implemented by teachers. A teacher at the school of architecture came up with the idea; it seemed to him that his students lacked any understanding of what it was that made Danish design world-famous in the years between 1930 and 1970. His students considered themselves to be artists, working for the sake of art only, as he put it. What was missing was the traditional cooperation with furniture makers and production people in general, to make them realise what was the exact purpose of their own work. He therefore contacted the other two institutions, starting a cooperation still existing today; however no longer with ASB as a participant. Since then, so many things have happened that a brief outline is called for, to explain the situation which forms the background for the way the subject area entrepreneurship is being taught.

From Product Development to Innovation and Entrepreneurship

In the next few years, the perspective of the subject area changed into "innovation and entrepreneurship". These two concepts were acquiring a special status as a number of influential players sought to further an emerging

P.C. van der Sijde et al. (eds.), *Teaching Entrepreneurship.*
© Physica-Verlag Berlin Heidelberg 2008

trend in society. Among other things, the rectors of the HE institutions, representatives from the local authority and the county along with the private institution Danish Technological Institute had visited Chalmers University of Technology in Gothenburg and learned about their successful initiative of offering graduate engineers courses in entrepreneurship just before they left the university. Though greatly inspired by the visit, they failed to reach any agreement on how to implement the idea in Aarhus. So it was parked in the Centre for Business Development (CBD), an office for business services run by the county. Each HE institution, the ones already mentioned plus the University of Aarhus, appointed a representative. At twice-yearly meetings they discussed developments and how to promote entrepreneurship at the individual institution. CBD offered courses in entrepreneurship at the university, the engineering college and the school of architecture, which was given additional funds for its own initiatives. ASB declined the offer as it was felt that the school was capable of developing and implementing this subject area on its own. This resulted in the course "Innovation & entrepreneurship", which has been offered ever since as part of the bachelor programme, alongside the inter-institutional projects mentioned above, referred to as TIP projects. The course was organised so that students could take the course in their fifth semester, then choose a TIP project cooperating with designers and engineers for their bachelor thesis in their sixth semester. But the teachers involved never succeeded in having a formalised framework set up, which meant that the process was difficult to manage, and not always a success. The Danish Rectors' Conference nevertheless granted approximately 60,000 € in 1993 to support the initiative, in order to further inter-disciplinarity. In 2003, ASB left the cooperation because it proved difficult to keep to the original idea alive once new teachers took over. Only one teacher from ASB was ever involved in the cooperation, and nobody else was willing to take over his commitment and hard work.

Promotion of Entrepreneurship

The meetings in CBD did not lead to more cooperation, as CBD had its own reasons for offering courses at the institutions. The courses were part of their business foundation and a means to attract funds from the initiatives set up by the Danish government. In 1995 the government launched a massive campaign to promote entrepreneurship. It did produce some results, but not in any coordinated way, usually as a result of a few passionate individuals' hard work and dedication. Some, but not a lot of progress was made up to 2000. In 1999 ASB started a master programme in "entrepreneurship", run jointly by teachers from the University of Aarhus and ASB, and a course in "Creativity and innovation management" was offered at the master programme. Since 1989 very few staff members at ASB have been involved in research on entrepreneurship. In 1997 a research group called RESME (Research on SMEs and Entrepreneurship) was established, including researchers and teachers from other universities and HE institutions.

Center for Entrepreneurship

However, 2001 finally marked a real change. The head of CBD organised a study tour to the USA for the members of the HE representatives. The tour included visits to Stanford and a number of other places. It was during this trip that the idea of establishing a centre in Aarhus comprising all HE institutions and supported by the county and local authority was formed: "Aarhus – one campus for entrepreneurship". The idea was immediately taken up by the administrative head of the county's business section. He managed to raise close to € 800,000 from the EU's Social Fund, whose administration was also placed in his organisation, and he managed to raise an equivalent sum from other sources as a grant to finance the Centre for Entrepreneurship (CFE) for three years, starting on 1 January 2002 and expiring at the end of 2004.

But the flying start was followed by a long and incredibly complicated process of negotiations: it soon emerged that there were many different agendas involved here. One of the most important turned out to be that the head of the county's business section needed to cut his staff and budget and saw the CFE as an opportunity to place his staff elsewhere, in an institution pursuing a good cause, and outside his budget. The teacher/researcher representatives from ASB and Aarhus University wanted the centre to be managed by the six HE institutions in Aarhus, and to be based on both research and education. They found that what was being suggested was far from the idea born out of the trip to the USA. The ensuing struggle went on and on until August 2002. CFE was officially opened on 1 December 2002 – one year into the budget period! The management of the centre was placed in the hands of staff from the county, and an academic council consisting of teacher representatives from the by then six institutions associated was set up. The centre attracted an impressive board, made up of the rectors of six institutions and executives from the local authority and county departments for business development. A number of adjustments were made over the next two years but nothing that changed the fundamental state of affairs. The centre had many visitors, who were, however, often disappointed because the centre was not what they expected, a centre for research and education. There was no agreement on the direction in which the centre was supposed to develop. In the end, the centre was made part of Aarhus University, governed by its rector as an ordinary staff function, disconnected from both the university's research and education in the subject area. Today, the centre has no importance for the development of entrepreneurship in education at ASB.

Inter-Disciplinary and Inter-Institutional Cooperation

This historical background has been included to illustrate the basic idea that has always been the driving force behind all development of subjects and courses for the person(s) responsible for this type of courses: that inter-disciplinarity is vital when teaching entrepreneurship. The course (see next page) was launched as cooperation between two teachers from the university and ASB, involving students from the many institutes and subject areas covered by the two institutions. For example students from the Institute of Molecular Biology, who took the course as part of their study programme. For the last two years, the course has been offered at ASB with an intake of 40–50 students a year; in 2006 students from ASB as well as other universities and HE institutions in Jutland, in 2007 students from ASB only. Over the past two years, a lot of resources have been devoted to restructuring the universities in Denmark. ASB has merged with Aarhus University, for example. The restructuring is the result of some degree of political pressure on HE institutions, in an effort to create new constellations in educational development and critical mass in research.

Course Design

Educational Approaches and Teaching Methods

The course "Entrepreneurship – from opportunity to action – the entrepreneurial process" is described on the next page.

Course description: Entrepreneurship - from opportunity to action - the entrepreneurial process

Relations to other Courses

The course is related to most of the courses taught in business studies. The course forms a good basis for participation in the Venture Cup, which starts officially at the same time as the course and runs parallel with the third and fourth semester of the master programme. The first phase ends in January with a prize of DKK 10,000 awarded to the best business plan. More information at www.venturecup.dk.

Aim of the Course

During as well as after their studies, many students will be involved in business development within existing organizations or they may wish to start their own business. The aim of the course is to give the students the intellectual tools to approach such tasks and to give them insight into and competences in entrepreneurship in practice through own projects and reflection on the projects. It is an integrated part of the course aim that the students contribute towards the creation of learning situations that further the competences required to fulfil the aim of both this specific course and of the study area in general – i.e., the development of 'enterprising behaviour'

Background of the Course

The background of the course is the well-established fact that there is a widespread need for innovation and entrepreneurship in the European economy; and Denmark is no exception. The study area aims not only to motivate and educate students to start their own business but generally to develop a certain kind of behaviour, referred to in literature as enterprising behaviour – a concept which in a Danish context was first used in Bang & Olufsen's vision statement in 1925.

Main Topics of the Course

The key objective of the course is to identify and clarify various elements of the concept 'entrepreneurship' through the students' own projects based on field studies. These projects will enable the students to carry out and understand the various elements characterising 'the entrepreneurial process' or method, from 'pre-idea to start-up', including:

- analysis of own competences in order to establish limitations and need for input of external resources
- carrying out sector/business analyses to spot potential for entrepreneurial activity
- investigating why, when and how business opportunities arise
- achieving an understanding of how such opportunities can be utilized
- demonstrating how the entrepreneurial process can transform a business opportunity into a business idea
- demonstrating a sense of reality when transforming a business idea into action.

The course, its methods and contents, is based on three essential concepts or philosophies. They are (a) entrepreneurial behaviour, (b) the entrepreneurial process, and (c) the student's self-knowledge of their own competences in relation to carrying out entrepreneurial processes. As for (a), it is the course's objective to further the behaviour described in the course description. As for (b), the objective is that the student learns the entrepreneurial process, as it is described under Main topics. It is not a requirement that a business plan is drawn up. This phase is not part of the course as such; the important thing is that a business idea is developed, and that the concept of opportunity is fully understood. And finally it is essential that, under (c), the students are able to identify complementary competences needed for the execution of their idea. This is where the original interdisciplinary element comes in. It is a requirement and a necessity, that the students seek help and knowledge in areas where their own competences are insufficient. Groups formed voluntarily tend to be fairly one-sided in their professional orientation, and it is usually evident that this kind of parallel thinking is not the most productive.

Curriculum and Course Development

The skeleton of the course is a model developed by Shane (2003), presenting his understanding of the entrepreneurial process (see Fig. 1). The course is not designed to prepare the students to start their own business when they graduate. As stated before, the emphasis is on entrepreneurial behaviour. This means that students will be favourably disposed towards entrepreneurship.

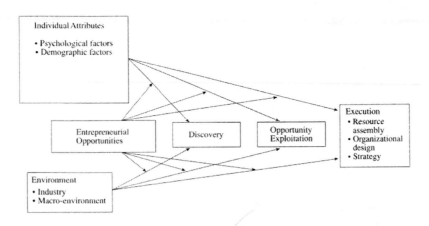

Fig. 1. A model of the entrepreneurial process. Source: Shane (2003)

The background for the pedagogical process is primarily Kolb's learning cycle (see Fig. 2).

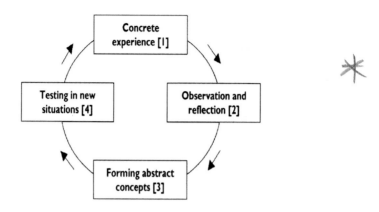

Fig. 2. Kolb's learning cycle. Source: Kolb (1984)

According to Kolb (see Blenker et al. 2006a, b) the learning illustrated in Fig. 2 is not really a circular process, but rather it is a matter of a cyclic spiral: firstly, it is often necessary to go through the four stages several times in order to fully understand the general principles. Secondly, it is more than a cycle, because you continually progress into a more profound discerning of the problem dealt with – as opposed to running in circles. Thus, learning to learn seems an important aspect in entrepreneurship since an entrepreneur frequently deals with entirely new business concepts and therefore cannot always seek advice or guidance in his network. Hence, it is necessary to experiment on your own; and it is far from certain that your initial, immediate understanding of the situation and the ensuing proposal for a solution will be accurate. You develop experience, and you learn to learn.

Learning Styles

In addition to recommending a cyclic experience-based learning process, the model can be expanded to encompass a representation of the way different people adopt different learning styles (see Fig. 3).

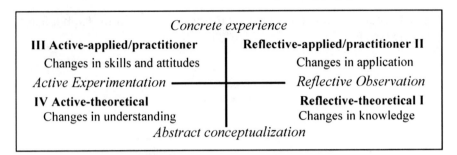

Fig. 3. Conceptual grid of learning styles

The quadrants of the cycle illustrate the four learning styles: concrete experience, reflective observation, abstract conceptualisation and active experimentation. The 'reflective theorist' will change the student's knowledge of the field: he acquires the knowledge material and seeks to conform to what has been learned. The learned material is adopted like a manual for the individual's activities. By applying the next learning style, 'the reflective practitioner', the learner obtains changes in the way of performing an action. This is about guidelines and advice yielding experience during a sequence of actions. The third learning style is 'the active practitioner'. According to this division, the learner will undergo a change in skills and in his attitude towards entrepreneurship: he adapts. Finally, there is the fourth learning style, 'the active theorist'. During the learning process the learner explicates or changes his perception of the phenomenon. He is the one who gathers the threads towards an understanding of what he is involved in. If we investigate how this division of learning styles fits in with entrepreneurship and entrepreneurs, Garavan and O'Cinneide (1994) refer to a series of studies showing that entrepreneurs prefer one of the active learning styles. Although, they say, practice shows that the teaching and training situation that potential entrepreneurs are most frequently exposed to is 'the reflective theorist'. This traditional teaching method is focused on developing the students' conceptual terminology, and the exam will be a matter of an ability to repeat these concepts. Learning participation is solely reflective (non-activating).

It has never been the intention to design the course and process to fit into a particular place in the model, but the model helps to give an understanding of where you are, and where you would like to be heading. Learning styles are not based on an outside-in understanding, but a concept associated usually with an individual and the way they learn. If you nevertheless try to place the course described somewhere in the model, it will be obvious that the course matches the 'conceptualization part' better than the 'application part'. Even if it has been the intention to develop 'changes in skills and attitudes', the model would probably say that the course is closer to 'changes in understanding'.

Current Challenges

Teaching at a university is a very personal activity, closely connected with the teacher's research interests, interests in general, age, etc. Teaching is also influenced by the culture and conditions at the institute offering the educational activities. The ideal is cooperation based on shared attitudes towards development. The introductory description explaining the background for the educational activities chosen for the course "Entrepreneurship – from opportunity to action – the entrepreneurial process" describes a sequence of activities, from experimenting, crossing discipline barriers, promoting, and implementing. Lots of things are happening on the entrepreneurial front in Aarhus. But there is no integration in the curricular programme, unless the students themselves make an effort and find the relevant actors – which, fortunately, they often do. Entrepreneurship is still immensely popular. Only, for the time being, there is no room for it in the regular educational activities at universities and HE institutions. Entrepreneurship is an extracurricular activity.

References

Blenker P, Dreisler P, Kjeldsen J (2006a) Entrepreneurship Education – the New Challenge Facing the Universities – A Framework for Understanding and Development of Entrepreneurial University Communities (Working Paper). Aarhus School of Business. Aarhus, Denmark

Blenker P, Dreisler P, Færgemann HM, Kjeldsen J (2006b) Learning and teaching entrepreneurship: Dilemmas, reflections and strategies. In Fayolle & Klandt (eds.) International Entrepreneurship Education: Issues and Newness, Cheltenham, UK, Edward Elgar

Garavan TN, O'Cinneide B (1994) "Entrepreneurship Education and Training Programmes: A Review and Evaluation – Part 1", J. Euro. Indust. Train., vol. 18 (8), 3–12

Kolb DA (1984) "Experiential Learning". New York: Prentice Hall, 1984

Shane S (2003) A General Theory of Entrepreneurship. The Individual-opportunity nexus. Cheltenham, UK, Edward Elgar

Teaching Entrepreneurship and Business Planning at Tallinn University of Technology

U. Venesaar

Tallinn School of Economics and Business Administration, Tallinn, Estonia

Background

Tallinn School of Economics and Business Administration (TSEBA) at Tallinn University of Technology (TUT) is one of the most important institutions of higher education in economics and business administration in Estonia. TSEBA offers study programmers at Bachelor, Master's and Doctoral level. Most of the economics courses to students in technical specialties at Tallinn University of Technology are provided by TSEBA. Programmes of the technical specialties at Tallinn University of Technology include two economic subjects such as (1) macro- and microeconomics and (2) business administration or entrepreneurship and business planning. The programme for students in technical specialties, as a rule on master's degree level, contains entrepreneurship and business planning as a compulsory subject. The objective is to improve students' knowledge about entrepreneurship, their skills for setting up a new business and to promote their entrepreneurial behaviour. Every year nearly 300 students take this course.

Changes in economic and social environment and moving towards an enterprising society have increased the significance of entrepreneurship studies on all levels of education. Fostering entrepreneurship among students has become an important topic in universities and governments as well as in research. The positive role of universities in developing entrepreneurial intention and to explore the factors influencing entrepreneurial behaviour of students is confirmed by a number of studies (Autio et al. 1997; Fayolle et al. 2005; Hannan et al. 2004). For Tallinn University of Technology the participation in Interreg IIIC programme project "Baltic Entrepreneurship

P.C. van der Sijde et al. (eds.), *Teaching Entrepreneurship.*
© Physica-Verlag Berlin Heidelberg 2008

Partners" (BEPART) has given an opportunity to exchange experiences between project partners and in cooperation with partners to develop entrepreneurship education at the university. The entrepreneurship teaching issues are directly discussed in a sub goal of the project: facilitation of high-quality and dynamic joint learning within the action-learning and reflection groups (ARG). Development of entrepreneurship education is supported by local political documents. A new entrepreneurship policy document in Estonia (2006–2013) is directed to the development of entrepreneurship and entrepreneurial initiative through a favourable entrepreneurship environment and appropriate support schemes. Activities in the following spheres are undertaken: entrepreneurship education in schools; life-long learning of the entrepreneurs; raising the awareness of entrepreneurship and innovation throughout the society; developing the ability of enterprises to co-operate. The role of Tallinn University of Technology is to develop entrepreneurship education for all specialties. The current case describes teaching entrepreneurship and business planning for students in technical specialties.

The Concept of Teaching Entrepreneurship and Business Planning

Entrepreneurship is viewed in general as a mindset and process to create and develop economic activity within a new or existing organization. Entrepreneurship is defined also as "… the nexus of two phenomena: the presence of lucrative opportunities and the presence of enterprising individuals" (Shane and Venkataraman 2000). These definitions refer to different perspectives on the level of entrepreneurial initiative in the country. In general we distinguish between factors related to a required external environment, and factors related to persons who have the motivation and capacity to identify and pursue business opportunities. The development of such motivated people, who have entrepreneurial competences, is an objective of Tallinn University of Technology.

Many researchers have evaluated the importance of entrepreneurial competency in connection with successful start-up and survival in business (Bird 2002; Onstenk 2003). The emphasis from the standpoint of educational institutions has been on providing a possibility of developing personal entrepreneurial competency (Bird 2002). In the view of Allan Gibb, the whole training programme should be oriented to learning and developing the skills needed to succeed in business. Consequently, instead of providing information and teaching in the style of traditional lectures, the main concept of entrepreneurial education is to support students' learning experiences via different learning models (e.g. 'learning by doing', 'project learning', 'problem-based learning' and 'action learning'). In Tallinn University of Technology the aim of learning for the students in technical specialities is to obtain knowledge in and for entrepreneurship as well as competencies in developing business ideas, finding business opportunities and going through the process of business planning. This teaching is based mainly on project based learning and enables students to learn by doing (e.g. practical work during the course in the process of writing business plan) and problem-based learning (e.g. solving problems that arise while implementing own business idea). The teachers' main tasks are to provide theoretical knowledge on entrepreneurship and business planning, to instruct the students to find and test business ideas, and assess business opportunities and to consult group work and business plan writing. The students should realise the importance of preparing a business plan, gain an overview of the Business Plan structure and preparation process, and get some practice in writing a business plan on the basis of their own business idea. Knowledge on how to implement a business idea, experience of business planning and information on the process of setting up an enterprise should motivate students to think about setting up their own business and as a result, bring more of them to entrepreneurship.

Course Description

The target group is primarily master's students in technical specialities, e.g. mechanics, chemistry, information technology, mathematics and natural sciences, power engineering, logistics etc. Depending on the economic subjects in their programmes, two different level groups can be distinguished. The combination of large numbers of students and relatively small numbers of classroom lessons creates a need for teaching methods that would provide the students with a comprehensive overview of the subjects of entrepreneurship and business administration and envisage that students prepare a business plan as an independent work task. The teaching is divided between classroom lectures and practical lessons. Theoretical lectures and principal discussions take place in large groups (approximately 70–150 students). Entrepreneurs from existing enterprises are invited in every lecture to speak about their experiences, problems and challenges in starting and running the business. The practical work of preparing business plans is conducted in practical classes in smaller rooms (up to 20 students). Development of a business idea and business plan writing are carried out as group work (approximately 2–4 students). Two teachers are involved. While one teacher is responsible for raising the students' awareness and providing knowledge on the theoretical side of entrepreneurship, business planning and business administration, the other is responsible for consulting students on business planning and writing business plans.

In classroom lessons the theoretical issues are taught. The use of active teaching methods and the involvement of students in the classroom work are limited due to the large audience. Hence, students listen to a lot of theoretical material in lectures, which is supplemented with many cases and real life examples from enterprises which can be discussed. Classroom lessons also discuss methodical methods that can be used in practical independent work outside the classroom (e.g. market research, collection of information on competitors, finding raw material and financial sources, etc.). In practical lessons discussions are held in smaller groups on different business planning subjects. Additionally, the subject is provided with the e-learning environment (Moodle), where the students find the lecture materials as well as instructions for practical work and tasks. The teachers and students can communicate, ask questions and have a discussion in the forum of e-learning environment. As a result, the students acquire practical experiences by evaluating the entrepreneurship environment and business opportunities, learn from experiences of existing enterprises, communicate with banks on credit raising terms, search a place for their potential enterprise etc. In brief, their business plan is born in real world considering the entrepreneurship environment in Estonia and opportunities for a new business to come to the market. As these are not real enterprises, however, a kind of game aspect remains. However, every year there are several students among the target groups at Tallinn University of Technology who make the business plan for themselves indeed with the purpose of starting their own business. The course comprises 16 lectures and 8 workshops.

Lectures

1. Introduction to the course. Business idea generation. Overview of the process and structure of business planning.
2. Entrepreneurship, entrepreneur, enterprise. The psychological portrait of the entrepreneur.
3. Recognition and evaluation of business opportunities. The mission, vision and aims of enterprise, business definition.
4. Internal and external environment of the enterprise.

5. Main principles of marketing. Market research. Product and price policy. Planning marketing policy.
6. Strategic analysis and development. Sales strategy and methods.
7. Business organisation and its legal forms. Non-profit organisations.
8. Establishment of a new enterprise, independent study on the basis of website http://www.aktiva.ee.
9. Accounting and recording. The structure of expenditures and accounting methods. Calculating net costs.
10. Profit statement. Cash flow prognosis. Balance.
11. Cost-benefit analysis.
12. Financial management and analysis. Time value of money.
13. Investment budgeting.
14. Entrepreneurship policy and business support system.
15. Entrepreneurship policy in Europe and measures for promoting SMEs.
16. Entrepreneur as a guest lecturer. Experience and suggestion on business start-up and business development issues.

Workshops

1. Consultation via e-mail or forums in issues of independent work: searching for and choice of a business idea, market research, analysis of factors that influence demand, collecting information on competitors. Independent work according to instructions and lecture materials in the e-study environment: conceiving and testing a business idea; evaluation of factors that influence demand; comparative table of competitors.
2. Discussion of the results of independent work in the development and implementation of a business idea: presentation of a business idea in groups, factors that influence demand, overview and comparative analysis of competitors; questions and answers.
3. Classroom consultation in general part of business plan related issues/ problems.
4. Defence of the general part of business plan with product/service pricing.
5. Consultation via e-mail in business plan related issues/problems, discussion and consultation if necessary in classroom.
6. Classroom consultation in business plan related issues/problems.
7. Seminar: analysis of cases/problems encountered in existing (operating) enterprises in Estonia and finding solutions to them. The analysis is based on newspaper or journal articles about real enterprises.
8. Defending business plans.

The course ends with a written examination. A precondition of being admitted to the examination is a timely submitted and positively defended business plan. The examination result is for 50% determined by the written examination and for 50% by the participation in classroom work and the business plan mark.

Current Challenges/Problems Facing the Organisation/ Project Experience or Educational Effort

The biggest challenge today is, that at the time the subject must be taken by a large number of students as a compulsory subject, which sets limits to using different active forms of teaching (e.g. action learning). Still, a quite suitable form for teaching large groups has been found in this case: the theoretical part in the form of lectures in a large group and practical lessons in smaller groups. The support of e-study helps a lot; it is a supplementary source of information for the students and a means of communication between themselves and with teachers. Learning of the subject is also facilitated by the website provided by the entrepreneurship support system, which contains examples and lessons from the life of enterprises in the business environment, and recommendations to other entrepreneurs.

Epilogue and Lessons Learned

Learning entrepreneurship and business planning by writing a business plan in real entrepreneurship environment enables to obtain a lot of knowledge on entrepreneurship problems and ways to solve them in real entrepreneurship environment. Co-operation with entrepreneurs is supporting students' attainment of practical knowledge about entrepreneurship and business planning. Such method will solve the problem of teaching in large groups, enabling the students to do practical work in smaller groups and learn by doing, and bringing the students as close to the real life as possible, and inciting them to work in search of possibilities to implement their own business idea. Such organisation of the teaching process contributes to the achievement of the objective: development of entrepreneurial behaviour of students and motivating them to start in business. Lessons learned from teaching in large groups of students indicate that in the future more co-operation in practice (e.g. enterprises, banks, entrepreneurship centres) will contribute to achievement of even better results in teaching the subject. It is important to expand cooperation between enterprises, public sector and university, and making this cooperation so effective that all parties involved remain interested in cooperation.

References

Autio E, Keeley RH, Klofsten M, Ulfstedt T (1997) Entrepreneurial Intent Among Students: Testing an Intent Model in Asia, Scandinavia and USA. Paper Presented at the Frontiers of Entrepreneurship Research, Wellesley, MA: Babson College. http://www.babson.edu/entrep/fer/papers97/autio/aut1.htm

Bird B (2002) Learning Entrepreneurship Competencies: The Self-Directed Learning Approach. *International Journal of Entrepreneurship Education*, 1, 203–227

Fayolle A, Gailly B, Lassas-Clerk N (2005) Capturing Variations in Attitude and Intentions: A Longitudinal Study to Assess the Pedagogical Effectiveness of Entrepreneurship Teaching Programmes. Working Paper of EMLYON of The European Institution for Life Long Learning, http://www.em-lyon.com

Hannan M, Hazlett SA, Leitch C (2004) Entrepreneurship Education: How Do We Measure Success? Working paper, Queen's University Belfast

Onstenk J (2003) Entrepreneurship and Vocational Education. *European Educational Research Journal*, 2, 74–89

Shane S, Venkataraman S (2000) The Promise of Entrepreneurship as a Field of Research. *Academy of Management Review*, 25, 217–226

References

Entrepreneurship Training for Innovative Start-Ups: The KTC Case

P. Milius[*] and J. Sarkiene

KTU regional Science Park, Kaunas, Lithuania

Introduction

Promotion of enterprise is one the principal goals of economical growth, as the main tasks of the development of the country – training of human resources, encouragement of scientific and technological advancement as well as innovations and intellectualisation, expedition of the GDP and reduction of social-economical exclusion among regions. All this can be achieved by being engaged in the intense development of a network of small and medium enterprises (SMEs). The development of SMEs is inseparable from commercialisation of innovations, cooperation between small and large companies as well as science and business, an effective infrastructure of business promotion, all of which influence economy and scientific development of the entire country. The primary conditions for SME development, as well as enterprise are knowledge, financial resources and an environment that initiates the growth and development of companies. Where knowledge is concerned, the emphasis should be on dissemination of information on entrepreneurship and access to training, consultancy and finance. These conditions are the essence of strategic development of SMEs.

Considering recommendations of the European Committee and experts as well as the present situation in the country, new means of promotion of entrepreneurship are currently planned, which will be financed from the state budget and the European Union Structural Funds – they are so called science valleys, complex programmes, national science programmes, and highly advanced science centres. The support will be available for lecturers and scientists, who are willing to improve their academic and pedagogical

P.C. van der Sijde et al. (eds.), *Teaching Entrepreneurship.*
© Physica-Verlag Berlin Heidelberg 2008

competence, also for the most productive groups of scientists. In order to achieve a better competitive ability of Lithuanian business, there is a need for initiatives to establish more scientific enterprises, to introduce new technologies, and make companies more effective. According to members of the Confederation of Industrialists, the country must pursue an integral policy when creating a better climate in the society, striving for intellectual nurturance (not only based on entrepreneurship) just by teaching citizens of the country, but also by removing obstacles for the establishment of new enterprises. A National Programme of Promotion of Youth Entrepreneurship for 2007–2011 (hereinafter called Programme) is currently implemented. Regarding entrepreneurship the following priorities are formulated:

- To strengthen the training of entrepreneurship of youth and aim at a larger number of people to start their own business as it is indicated in the Government programme of 2004–2008.
- Strategic documents of the Republic of Lithuania highlight entrepreneurship as one of the principal factors of a balanced growth of the economy and regional development together with knowledge, capital and labour force.
- In the field of education, the regulations of the state educational strategy for 2003–2012 intend to enhance the attention for entrepreneurship at all levels of education.
- A lifelong learning strategy aims at establishing conditions to train entrepreneurship as one of the main skills in the lifelong learning context in the entire system of education (including the informal one). The activity plan of this strategy focuses on the creation and implementation of continuous vocational study programmes, which concentrate on general abilities (including entrepreneurship) and vocational training, and evaluate social and economical as well as regional demands.
- In the context of the Lithuanian labour market, the long-term strategy for the country's development perceives entrepreneurship as a political means, whereas the strategy of vocational guidance aims at applying the training of entrepreneurship into the system of vocational guidance and consulting.
- One of the most important strategic policies planned for the country's SMEs until 2008, is improving the human resources through formal and informal education, consultancy and training, focused on economical, managerial, financial, accounting, marketing, and legal competencies.

- A Lithuanian common programming document for the promotion of entrepreneurship as a priority – as training of a skill and as promotion for business.
- There are enough programmes, strategies and initiatives for training of entrepreneurship in Lithuania, however, the majority of these are not based on own experience – learning by doing.

The KTU Regional Science Park

The KTU Regional Science Park (KTC) is part of the programme of state promotion for SMEs, which aims at:

- Promoting entrepreneurship in the field of high technologies as well as technology transfer processes between science and industry.
- The creation of a favourable environment for business and innovations.
- The application of scientific and technological achievements for regional development.
- The development of competitive companies.
- Incentives to establish new businesses and work places (see Fig. 1).

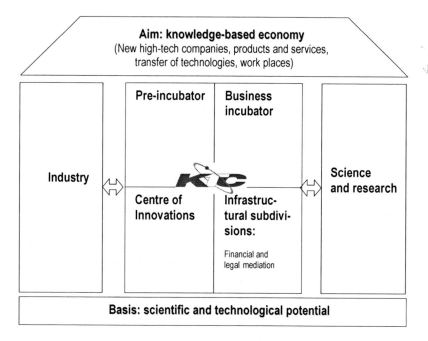

Fig. 1 Structure of KTC

KTC is the first structure of this kind in Lithuania. It consists of a:

- Pre-incubator: a structure where business ideas can be 'incubated' and tested. The main users of pre-incubators are university post-graduates, scientists and specialists, who do research in relevant business sectors and search for opportunities to start their own business by commercialising the results of research.
- Business incubator (business development centre): a traditionally operating structure, which incubates enterprises and offers them all the necessary services needed for start-up. The prospective group of users are technologically and innovatively oriented companies, 'spin-outs' and 'spin-offs', that have passed the pre-incubatory period.
- Centre of innovations with as main functions the technological audit, issues of protection of intellectual property, patenting, and monitoring as well as transfer of technologies.
- Science Park is the link between all elements in the structure. The science park houses high-tech and innovative companies. The purposive group of clients – companies leaving the business incubator, 'spin-off' and 'spin-out' companies of universities and industrial enterprises, operating in similar fields and, according to their activity profile, capable of forming a cluster. The Science Park also offers financial and legal services.

One of the main aims of KTC is also to promote entrepreneurship in the Kaunas Region via training.

KTC Entrepreneurship Training

In order to start business it is not enough to have a great business idea and a wish to implement it as fast as possible. Starting a business is a complex and complicated process that consists of several stages: the business idea (it is a determination of a niche and product (service) to fulfil that niche), evaluation of a entrepreneur's personal features as well as conditions of business organisation, selection of a company's legal form, preparation of a business plan, and registration of a company. One of the first activities to start business is scanning exploration of a business environment for the precise possibilities and the competitors. Practically there are three important factors determining a successful activity of a company: the (business) idea, the entrepreneurial competences and the financial potential.

Considering the different needs for training among those willing to start their own business and the ones already having it, training sessions in the science park have been divided into two groups and a programme of entrepreneurship training has been established. This programme consists of four parts (see Fig. 2): motivation for innovative entrepreneurship, training on innovative entrepreneurship, participation in activities of international and national networks and partnership and implementation of projects. The first training cycle is more oriented towards demands of knowledge on entrepreneurship of potential entrepreneurs (baccalaureates and postgraduates). The target group of the second training cycle of entrepreneurship programme – heads and managers of young companies as well as all others who are thinking of establishing their own business. The aim of this training programme is to encourage young companies to be more active, take risks, base their activities on innovations, apply the newest and most advanced technologies, help find and exhibit the strongest personal characteristics, and thus contribute to entrepreneurship promoting in Kaunas Region.

- Traditional assistance for young innovative companies:
  - lease of administrative/office premises in KTC under favourable conditions; various services,
  - consultations on issues of business start,
  - forms of financial promotion for business starters,
  - assistance in preparation for and participation in national and international exhibitions.
- Entrepreneurship training programme:
  - programme of motivation of innovative entrepreneurship,
  - programme of training of innovative entrepreneurship.
- Participation in activities of international and national networks including initiatives of technological platforms and clusters.
- Partnership and implementation of international and national projects.

Fig. 2 KTC actions/activities promoting entrepreneurship in Kaunas Region

KTC has been organising training sessions for business starters since 1999. An idea to create a systematic, purposeful and regular training programme emerged in 2004, after the need of such trainings had been noticed. Every year the entrepreneurship training programme is improved, renewed and offered to learners, using contemporary innovative training methods. This programme was created by the administrative staff of the science park (director and liable managers) together with research workers and lecturers of Kaunas University of Technology (KTU). Individual seminars of the training programme are conducted by KTC staff, though the majority of training sessions are conducted by KTU lecturers who have the necessary knowledge and experience. Experienced entrepreneurs are invited to share their experiences. Sharing of practical experience is one of the fastest and most efficient ways to promote entrepreneurship and business. The programme of motivation for innovative entrepreneurship (see Table 1) induces not only the establishment of commercial enterprise, but also trains the (personal) skills to use all opportunities and set up the company according to their personal visions.

Table 1 The KTC programme of motivation of innovatory entrepreneurship

Criteria	Description
Course Nb. and hours	6 courses, 48 academic hours
Entrance criteria	–
Programme structure	• Basics of innovative entrepreneurship • Creative thinking • Entrepreneurship and the dynamics of the environment • Entrepreneurship and leadership • SME promotion • Exchange of experience with experienced entrepreneurs
Course time schedule	Once a week/6–8 h
Number of participants	8–12 (max 15) participants

It is a programme, which supplements a personal 'competence portfolio' with knowledge and encourages participants of the training sessions to change the status quo themselves. Many people have different thoughts and activity ideas, though they are incapable of identifying activity priorities. The aim of the cycle of these motivation trainings – to help understand what kind of activity would motivate and promote entrepreneurship, i.e. train skills, assist in finding different possibilities, raise motivation as well as attitudes of a young man, and introduce the available promotion in the process of establishing and developing business.

The programme of training of innovative entrepreneurship (see Table 2) provides theoretical and practical knowledge on marketing, financial recruitment, management of new and just-starting companies, and training of the culture of organisation and creativity of personnel as well as development of business based on scientific researches and experiments.

Table 2 The programme of training of innovatory entrepreneurship in KTC

Criteria	Description
Course Nb. and hours	10 courses, 80 academic hours
Entrance criteria	–
Programme structure	1. Entrepreneurship, innovation, intrapreneurship 2. Innovation and knowledge management. Innovation policy. Technology transfer between science and business enterprises 3. Business planning and development. Tech nology strategy methodology and business 4. Marketing strategies. Business internationalisation 5. Project management 6. Financing possibilities of innovative enterprises 7. Human Resource Management. Motivation. Leadership 8. Organisational culture and management 9. Intellectual Property Rights. Licensing 10. Stories of success and practical advice
Course type/used methods	Courses are based on group/team work, active training methods, video material, and discussions
Course time schedule	Once a week/6–8 h
Number of participants	8–12 (max 15) participants

The programme is based on the concept that knowledge should be acquired not only in a seminar, but also communicating directly with experienced entrepreneurs, participating in practical trainings of nurturing entrepreneur's personality and character, analysing practical situations, modelling business, and working in teams. Besides, the programme contributes greatly to the improvement of quality of business plans from the growing number of projects from different sources (business angel networks, venture capital funds, programmes of municipalities and business promotion agencies). Business plans, prepared in the process of trainings, can be implemented in KTC. In order to create the programme of training of innovatory entrepreneurship international experience in the fields of entrepreneurship training and promoting was taken as the basis, which is believed to have greatly influenced the demand and efficiency of entrepreneurship trainings, as compared with analogous entrepreneurship training and promoting programmes, currently existing in the market. This training programme contributes to the development of knowledge-based business, establishment of new companies (especially in the priority fields of high technologies), their internationalisation, creation and commercialisation of new products, and strengthening of links between science and business.

Current Challenges

In pursuit of the policy of the rapid development of integrated economy it is vital to create a favourable climate for entrepreneurship training in the society, aiming at a change of mindset as well as at improvement of skills and elimination of obstacles of establishment and development of new companies. Considering this, next to the discussed and pending problems of regulation, taxes and finances, it is advised to create and apply horizontal means for the establishment of promotion basis of the entrepreneurship policy. In order to more efficiently organise processes of entrepreneurship motivation and training as well as its development in the activities of science parks it is important to consider and evaluate properly such processes like organisation of innovative business, purposeful investment and constant training.

Innovation and entrepreneurship are not always interconnected. Due to insufficiently close cooperation among scientific research institutions, universities and businessmen in the fields of researches and creation of new products and technologies for the market, businessmen do not always find innovations attractive. Usually the fields of scientific research pass business demands and a lack of results suitable for commercialisation is felt. Therefore, one of the most important tasks in this field is to train entrepreneurship not merely among companies that apply innovation practically, but also among scientists and researchers. This would significantly increase the relevance of scientific researches towards business, would encourage researchers and scientist to be more active while implementing tasks of technological development, and choosing research subjects, international experience and databases would be employed.

Entrepreneurship training and investments in innovations are essential not only for high-tech companies, but also in branches of traditional industry and service sector. An innovatory attitude towards business management and a constant application of innovations contribute to improve labour productivity, efficiency, quality, and at the same time international competitive ability of a company. Considering the low level of innovative activity of the country's companies, it is essential to intensively stimulate creative innovative activity, i.e. intensify cooperation between business and scientific research institutions, induce the development of research done by companies and support the establishment of technical facilities necessary for this kind of activity. It should be mentioned that there are cases when heads of Lithuanian companies do not know that they have some problems, which impede the development of a successful business, therefore it is important to help find them. Entrepreneurship trainings, organised by institutions of the network of public services to business, are often very helpful in solving problems of the lack of knowledge or skills. Thus, accessibility of public services to business, its content and quality, conformity with demands of business companies and business starters, is an important factor to raise the level of entrepreneurship.

A lot of national and regional means are often initiated on the basis of priorities stated in EU or national programmes. When implementation period of these programmes is over and new ones appear, the further pursuance of these initiatives is usually intermitted. Therefore, consultation services and training cycles are often unfinished. As a result, when forming entrepreneurship training programmes, it is essential to project their continuation after financial resources end up. Application of innovations to business is basically done as adaptation of necessary technologies, but not as creation of original knowledge or application of somewhere else created innovations. Only the national and European long-term promotion can be helpful in creating and applying strategically advanced innovations practically. The Lithuanian system of means of financial promotion for SMEs is not fully developed. Credit institutions are not very active in granting micro-credits for business starting companies, there is a passive activity of venture capital funds in the field of sponsorship of projects created by young innovative companies. Innovations are always related with big risk, therefore, due to the over-risky projects, banks often refuse to finance them. In foreign countries informal individual investors – 'business angels' – come to help. They are ready to invest their capital in risky businesses just appealing to their experience and interests. In Lithuania the real 'business angels' still do not exist, because there are not many people who freely hold the sums bigger than € 100,000, thus, only unification of 'business angels' can be discussed. Notably, the demands of modern business are bigger than business patrons can offer. Businessmen need to be prepared for management of investments, since the expenditures, necessary for doing innovative activity, are planned easily, but the income is not. Many businessmen lack financial resources to order investment projects at experienced companies, thus, trainings that focus on practical preparation are relevant and necessary. Such training sessions allow businessmen to prepare investment projects on their own with the help of consultants. It should not be strange if university graduates become initiators of innovative enterprises. The data of various researches show that graduates of universities already do start their own business; however, universities should aim at making entrepreneurship an important part of their curricula and introduce entrepreneurship-based competencies in science and technical studies, so students and researchers will have an opportunity to better commercialise their own ideas as well as develop new technologies. Entrepreneurship training in universities and schools should be integrated into programmes of technical disciplines. This establishes better conditions for 'spin-offs' and innovatory companies to appear and helps scientific researchers gain entrepreneurship skills. Spin-offs – companies that were established on the basis of researches done by higher education schools – are more often emphasised as a means of strengthening the development of local economy. However, their rates of establishment and development are very dependent on scientists' entrepreneurship abilities. Due to some inner barriers, like a system of career, which is built on academic achievements, the entrepreneurship of the latter at universities is not appreciated positively. It is very important to have the necessary number of lecturers to teach entrepreneurship.

Having evaluated Lithuanian scientific potential, it can be stated that only a minor part of modern technologies, which are necessary for Lithuanian companies, can be created in Lithuania. This means that Lithuanian companies will have to purchase the vast majority of modern and competitive technologies in other countries. The rise of such tendencies has already been noticed. To purchase foreign technologies and apply them in our companies is a more complex task than to do the same with local technologies. Often such a task is too complicated for Lithuanian SMEs, which lack experience in international cooperation, transfer of intellectual property and application of technologies. Here, the role of science parks and centres of innovation is very significant, as are their international contacts and assistance for firms when applying for FP-7, COST, Eureka, and other EU programmes.

Conclusions

One of the principal aims of the policy on SME development of the Government of Lithuania is to establish favourable conditions for new companies to appear and to increase the rates of successfully working companies as well as their competitive abilities. This requires government institutions to constantly observe and consider dynamically changing situations of business companies, to review, improve and/or foresee new means of promotion, development and inducement as well as long-term programmes for the further development of entrepreneurship in the country. The government, implementing the programme of SME development, needs to cooperate, i.e. be in a continuous relation with companies and consider entrepreneurs' opinions on the contemporary business environment in the country, to evaluate present and rising problems and obstacles of business development, and on their basis to set actions in the direction of making the applied means more efficient. As a result of such a constant contact between government institutions and business representatives, the level of entrepreneurship in the country should rise.

An entrepreneurship training system has been established and is practically applied in all levels, from primary school to university. It has been conceived that schoolchildren should get information on entrepreneurship from an early age. They should be taught about it as a possible future occupation. Moreover, the main skills of entrepreneurship and creativity should be trained, as well as self-confidence in any activity. Universities must include principles of entrepreneurship into their curricula as an important part of training programmes and encourage or even demand students to choose the courses in entrepreneurship. An insufficient level of entrepreneurship in the society is one of the main problems of development of SMEs. It should be solved by pursuing the state's integrated policy, covering the promotion of entrepreneurship-based attitude by coherent training and teaching of all as well as the elimination of obstacles of business establishment and development. Entrepreneurship training increases the possibilities of the establishment of new, sustainable companies.

Advancing Business Planning: From Planning to Entrepreneurial Learning

P. Kyrö[*] and M. Niemi

Helsinki School of Economics, Helsinki, Finland

Introduction

The benefits of business planning and our abilities to teach it have recently been questioned from both practical and theoretical perspectives. Carrier (2005), claims that instead of conducting the traditional business planning, we should be more creative and, in teaching, too, focus more on inventing and developing business ideas. Hindle (1997) also criticises the standardised form of business planning and demands more flexibility and creativity instead of rigidity. The benefits of planning might actually rather be a myth than a fact, since planning does not necessarily improve performance. Tomas Karlsson (2005) argues that there is actually only a tenuous relationship between planning and performance. He also suggests that there is no evidence that the performance of a start-up business will improve or have more potential if the entrepreneur has made a business plan. The situation may even be the opposite, as Carter, Gartner and Reinold's (1996) study indicated. Those having a business plan in their early start-up phase tended to stay in the intention phase longer than others. Thus, instead of helping to start the business, business planning seems rather to cause more or less delay in this process. Delmar and Shane (2004) also discovered that there was no significant relationship between the writing of a business plan and subsequent profitability. Regardless of these problems, recent Western reports indicate that the most popular approach to teaching entrepreneurship in universities is business planning (Menzies 2005).

So basically, it is quite reasonable to ask why we teach and carry out business planning if it does not help us to start a business or to improve our business performance. To combine creativity and business planning,

P.C. van der Sijde et al. (eds.), *Teaching Entrepreneurship.*
© Physica-Verlag Berlin Heidelberg 2008

however, seems to be an unknown and sometimes contradictory territory in teaching. For example, Fiet (2001) and Tienne and Chandler (2004) admit that it is possible to teach opportunity recognition, but, for instance, Saks and Gaglio's (2002) exploratory research provides quite contradictory results. In-depth interviews of 14 well-known entrepreneurship teachers ended up to the conclusion that it is possible to teach opportunity evaluation, but rather difficult, if not impossible, to teach opportunity recognition, not to mention creation. However, nearly three-quarters of the respondents hoped the students would in fact be able to learn to identify potential business ideas. Carrier (2005) argues that this actually is the problem of teaching business planning; we should be more creative and put more emphasis on creating the business idea, in stead of evaluating existing ideas. These research results on the significance and role of business planning in practice and teaching indicate that we have problems both in the models and in teaching business planning. In both of them the collide focuses on the contradiction between creativity and planning. To combine these in conceptual models and their teaching seems to be the unsolved problem, which is deeply embedded in the very paradigm of planning and teaching.

Thus we suggest that the problem might be in the configuration approach and its paradigm that rather relies on dualism and linear modelling than innovative and complex human intelligence. In order to concretize these problems and advance in finding solutions to them we apply the methods of concept mapping and intelligent soft computing and provide a new business plan modelling that simultaneously considers the modelling and learning aspects of business planning. We do this by employing a constructive research approach.

The Constructive Research Approach

Lukka (2001) has developed a constructive research method for this kind of problem solving. He argues that the basic nature of constructive research approach concerns problem solving, which at the same time provides solutions as an interplay between practice and theories and reaches a more profound epistemological level of knowledge creation. Instead of using decision-oriented approach to problem solving, constructive approach relies on heuristic innovations. "The ideal result of a constructive research project is that a real-world problem is solved by an implemented new construction, which has both great practical and theoretical contribution"

(Lukka 2001). By following this approach we first summarise the problems of traditional business planning revealing the practical problem – of teaching and learning business planning – with potential for theoretical contribution. Then by reflecting on the criticism levelled at traditional business planning, we innovate a theoretical solution and the starting points and challenges for our modelling. This is followed by integrating the phases of innovating and developing the business idea into modelling. Then we will examine how to use concept mapping in identifying the phenomena and relationships in traditional business planning. By using these methods we further evaluate and develop the business idea by dividing and extending traditional modelling into three processes: transformation, traditional calculations and a start-up feasibility study with four aspects of evaluation. Finally, we will sum up our progress in the modelling and draw conclusions.

Table 1 Phases of the constructive research approach

Phases of constructive research approach	Learning business plan project
1. Find a practically relevant problem, which also has potential for theoretical contribution	Questioning the benefits of traditional business planning – need for a new configuration
2. Examine the potential for long-term research co-operation with the target organisation	Gathering partners and research group for the project
3. Acquiring a profound practical and theoretical understanding of the research area	– Analyzing existing business planning models – Analysing technical solutions and choosing the basic approaches – The process of searching for new solutions will continue throughout the project
4. Innovating theoretical solutions and the practical construction with potential for theoretical contribution	See Table 2
5. Implementing the solution and testing its functionality and usability	Heuristic usability evaluation of the pilot model
6. Identifying and analysing theoretical contribution	Embedded in every step of the research. To be reported in scientific articles and conference papers

Problems in Traditional Business Planning

The origin of business planning can be traced back to large companies' long term planning after World War II (Karlsson 2005). Drucker (1959) was among those who first introduced long term planning to entrepreneurship. Only in 1980s did scholarly literature on business planning begin to be published more extensively. It followed the ideal of the benefits of long term planning to business performance. This normative literature focused on teaching how strategic decisions lead to operational functions and further to practical calculations (Robinson 1979). Only at the end of 1990s did we start to question its effectiveness and usability in improving business performance (Hindle 1997; Karlsson 2005). As Karlsson (2005) argues, the literature on business planning is somewhat homogenous and follows certain rules. Hindle (1997) also found that the business planning literature was normative and that its paradigm did not provide a consistent body of theoretical justification for its boundaries, laws and success rules. According to him, it seems clear that many of the business planning authors have read one another, but nevertheless there is very little cross-referencing in the business planning literature. As he puts it: "Every author is a virtual world unto himself or herself" (Hindle 1997). Hindle also notes that the main aim of traditional business planning has been attracting equity investors instead of developing entrepreneurs' own business ideas. Thus the focus has been on writing a plan that is convincing from the investors' point of view. Hindle (1997) summarises the problems of the business planning paradigm in three rules. The first the "keep it short" rule requires that regardless of the plan it should be limited to 40 pages because venture capitalists do not have time to read long business plans. The second criticism concerns the rule "employ a standard table of contents" though, as he argues, integrating the relevant components into the business plan requires flexibility and creativity, not rigidity. A standardised table of contents can lead to reductionism, not integration. The third "do it yourself" rule assumes that the potential entrepreneurs can manage alone in businesses planning.

Our findings from analysing the existing business planning literature concur with Hindle's findings. After reading and categorising a wide range of available books and articles we chose examples of each category for further analysis (Alanärä 2004). Thus we had as standard models four international books, two international articles, two Finnish working manuals and three international simulation models. Despite their similarity, there were some differences between these. The main attention was paid to existing product/service or product improvement. However, the models did not leave room for the innovative and unique development of products or services. Competition was also analysed as a static cross-section of the current situation. Thus, although setting aims and pondering strategies were encouraged, the main interest was in operational aspects. Only three out of these ten examples paid attention to entrepreneurs' individual competences, two to the entrepreneur's financial situation, but none to creating and developing the business idea or to the aspects of motivation and volition. Combining our observations with Hindle's findings provides three main categories of the core features of the traditional business planning which also include its limitations and problems.

1. Business planning is regarded as an objective, isolated phenomenon excluding individual competences and contribution as well as creativity, motivation and volition, thus also excluding individual and contextual factors and processes as well as innovativeness.
2. Its normative and static form follows a linear and rational logic and focuses on an existing idea and situation also excluding innovative learning and development.
3. It assumes that business planning and consequently learning is a static and functional series of operational planning activities.

These core features of business planning are contradictory to those theories of entrepreneurship that stress the innovative abilities and processes, opportunity recognition, creation and exploitation of opportunities as well as the complex and complicated context of entrepreneurial processes. Thus our findings are parallel to the criticism levelled at business planning models and their teaching. They also justify Hindle's claim about the problems with the current paradigm and theoretical foundation of business planning. Karlsson's (2005), Carter et al. (1996) as well as Delmar and Shane's (2004) findings on the ineffectiveness of business planning may actually derive from these core features of traditional business planning and set business planning apart from the entrepreneurship theory discussion. This also justifies Carrier's (2005) criticism regarding the lack of creativity in teaching business planning. Thus in order to advance the modelling and teaching of business planning, we should be able to solve these two separate, but interrelated problems. First we need to find a way to model business planning that follows the core aspects and dynamics of entrepreneurial behaviour and processes. Then we should be able to find an approach to teaching it. For this purpose we apply concept mapping methods and the opportunities offered by intelligent soft computing. Next we present these efforts to solve each of the three problems of the current business planning models and thereafter our solution to teaching problems.

Changing the Paradigm from Planning to Individual Learning

To depart from normative planning and start from the individual, we first defined our ontological assumptions of human actor and action. In the entrepreneurial framework this refers to the human being who is a unique, holistic and creative individual capable of inventing and generating business ideas and activities in complex and complicated environments. This assumes that the model should also include the phases for creating and evaluating the business idea itself. Instead of starting from evaluating the existing business idea we have a five-phase model. Phase 1 entails evaluating the innovativeness of the business idea from an individual perspective. Phase 2 interacts with phase 1 by encouraging the learner to develop the idea further. Both of these are context bound linguistic, descriptive phases supported by graphical representations. Only in Phase 3 do we start to exploit in some respects the traditional concepts of evaluation and then proceed to implementation (Phase 4) and re-evaluation (Phase 5).

Creativeness and innovativeness relate to the opportunity recognition and new venture discussion in entrepreneurship research (Puhakka 2002; Timmons 1994). However, the concepts of creating and recognizing opportunities have been used almost synonymously. For example, Jones and Dimitratos (2003) define entrepreneurial creativity as recognizing opportunities for developing and exploiting resources. In the context of new venture creation Davidsson et al. (2002) differentiate the novelty of organic growth from growth in general. An example of an alternative definition is Yiu and Briggs's (2000) concept of creativity. For them it refers to the art of renewal and recreation. Thus conceptualising creativity and innovativeness is still quite unclear and problematic. To overcome this confusion we can learn from Eijnatten's idea of novelty. In the context of chaordic thinking he contrasts individual and collective entrepreneurial novelty with improvement. He suggests that if we know both the goal and path we can only make improvements, but if either of these is unknown we renew our practices, and finally, if both of these aspects are unknown, we can achieve real novelty. (Eijnatten 2005). This helps us to draw a distinction between creating, recognizing and finally imitating or depicting opportunities. We can suggest that knowing both the path and the goal refers to depicting a business idea. If we recognize something, it means that either the goal or the path is unknown and finally creating something refers to something non-existent, meaning that both the goal and the path are still unknown. We thus have three basic options and their different variations and degrees, viz. depicting, recognising and creating opportunities to be exploited. The differences between these three zones are explicated by the degrees of known and unknown. Even for each unique individual these concepts are relative, in business activities newness is also always a collective phenomenon evaluated by the clients. This means that the more creative the business idea, the more unknown it is to both its creator/s and those taking advantage of this creation, that is its potential clients. Consequently we regard client as a dimension, not only as a context. Together these three define the novelty of the product or service. Thus the degree of knowing defines three different zones of innovativeness, viz. depicting, recognising and creating with respect to its three dimensions, viz. goal, path and client (Fig. 1).

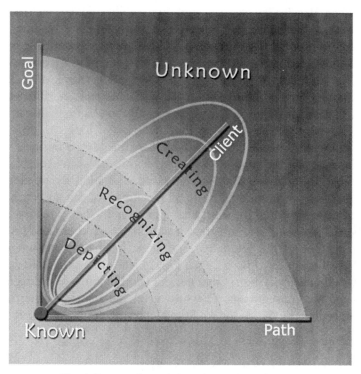

Fig. 1 Zones of creativity of a business idea

Creativity is individual ability, while innovativeness might refer to both the business idea and the ability of individual. Inventing a business idea relates essentially to an individual's abilities and readiness to exploit opportunities be s/he the entrepreneur or the client. Both of these should be anticipated. Nevertheless the innovativeness of any business idea should always be evaluated collectively, assuming that exploiting it requires many clients. The dynamics between different zones thus combine individual and collective experiences and readiness and can be anticipated through their external representations such as buying habits and preferences, values, income levels, demographic factors etc. Thus we can include some aspects of traditional business planning, such as market segmentation, in our modelling but still consider entrepreneurs' competences and readiness as key factors in creating and developing the business idea and in evaluating its success. In other words, we can in some respects overcome the problems of normative and quantitative evaluation of traditional business planning. Based on the three zones and their individual and collective assessment, anticipating the risk involved in exploiting a business idea assumes new dimensions. Besides the classical start-up feasibility studies, the risk-analyses also concern the individual aspects and entrepreneur's readiness for the exploitation process. To evaluate individual dimensions of this model and the risks involved in the start-up phase more generally, we can learn something, for example, from the logic of effectuation (Sarasvathy 2001a, b). By observing how entrepreneurs make decisions and act, Sarasvathy concludes that experienced entrepreneurs emphasize action instead of planning. They concentrate on what they have, what they can do, who they know and what is needed. On this basis they create new business ventures. Thus in assessing the success of the business ideas, such aspects should be considered. By applying this more versatile evaluation we are able to solve some problems of traditional business planning: we can approach it on the basis of entrepreneurial theories, treat it as an individually relative and context bound phenomenon, integrate it with innovativeness and break down the boundaries of the normative and static business planning paradigm. Based on these ideas, Phase 2 (see Fig. 2) leads to a linguistic description of a two-dimensional matrix that defines combinations of products (or services) and market segments. This now gives the learner the starting points for proceeding to the more traditional phases of the business planning process.

Concept Mapping as a Method

In order to deviate from the normative, linear and rational logic of traditional business planning, we applied the concept mapping method, which enables more complex and versatile modelling. In concept mapping the phenomena and their internal relationships are defined and revealed. This approach enables the learner to comprehensively understand the relations between the phenomena. At the same time, soft computing makes it possible to attach different entities under each concept and to produce a wide range of information on the whole. This also enables interplay between linguistic descriptions and numerical calculations.

Human thinking consists of the basic units of both concepts and images. According to Åhlberg (1990) it stands critical testing and corresponds to other theories and evidence we have about human thinking. Human beings are continuously constructing "maps" of the world both intentionally and without conscious intention to do so. We construct concept maps based on concepts and propositions and include our best explanations of why the observable world is as it is. Thus, conceptual maps are internal representations of the world (Åhlberg 1990). For each individual, the main elements of her/his thinking and unobservable cognitive structures, may be expressed as concept maps, which along with speaking and writing are external representations of mental internal representations. However, besides cognitive constructs of personality and intelligence, also conative and affective aspects are considered (Kyrö 2007). Concept maps present selectively only the most important aspects of our internal and/or external world or a part of it. If we add too many details to the map, it becomes impossible to read and thus useless (Åhlberg 1990, 1993). This fact gives us guidance for differentiating complex decision rules from the actual representation the learner faces. In our approach we use the improved concept maps presented by Åhlberg (2001). The viewpoints of the methodology are summarized hereafter.

All concepts are interpreted as main elements of thinking, and they are always inside frames. Sometimes concepts require many words in order to be correctly labelled. There is no exact limit for how many words may be included in a concept label. In an improved concept map you use as many words as are needed to name the concept accurately. Although most of the phenomena used in business planning and in business evaluation (see Fig. 2, Phase 4) already have quite specific definitions provided by the existing business planning literature, some concepts still have to be defined with several words. All links between concepts have an arrowhead to show in which direction the connection from one concept to another is to be read in order to produce a meaningful proposition. This is essential in our computational modelling, because the directions of relations describe whether phenomena are outputs from or inputs to other phenomena. In an improved concept map each concept only occurs once, just as in a good geographical map each place name is only found once. If each concept only occurs once on the concept map, then it is easy to count how many inputs each concept has from other concepts when we use methods of soft computing. Generally in the concept mapping method – and also in Åhlberg's improved concept mapping method – there are always linguistic descriptions connected to links. These expressions may be short or long. The essential point is that the link includes a verbal expression and the resulting proposition is meaningful and more or less true, plausible, probable etc. We might also use linguistic expressions in our conceptual maps in future. However, in our actual computational modelling of neuro-fuzzy maps we aim to reveal the quantitative relations connected to these links – this process will be invisible to the learner. As we advance in this modelling we will be able to solve problems using the exact numerical values (on a scale of 0–1) of relations when we use neuro-fuzzy reasoning in the evaluation process. Defining concepts is crucial for successful concept mapping, since, as Åhlberg (2001) states, all concepts are interpreted as main elements of thinking and the measure of validity is then how well the concept map corresponds to the thinking of the person. Moreover, the number of concepts should be reasonable but allow the learner to identify the essential phenomena and their relationships. In cognitive psychology some research findings indicate that the number of concepts should be limited to 5–7. Keeping both of these in mind we further divided Phase 3 into three separate phases (see Fig. 2).

The Five-Phased Model

As the evaluation of the business plan in Phase 3 is divided into three separate phases, the phases of implementation and re-evaluation are for now left out of this modelling. Traditional business planning gives instructions on the numbers and calculations, but mostly fails to advise how to produce them. Thus, the new sub-phases of the business plan evaluation are defined as follows: Phase 3 consists of transforming the linguistic description of the innovative idea into numerical form and helps the learner in this transformation process. Phase 4 involves producing traditional financial calculations and Phase 5 evaluates these results from four aspects both numerically and heuristically.

Soft computing can on the one hand solve the problems of the transformation process and on the other hand process the information fed into the system and produce different proposed decisions based on given decision-making rules. These proposed decisions enable a non-linear and comprehensive dialogue between the learner and the produced information. These together comprise the net of concepts and their relationships that allow the learner simultaneously to perceive how the essential concepts due to his/her actions change in their relationships. In our process of definition we integrated concepts of business planning, marketing and accounting with a heuristic evaluation of their meaning. This of course can and should be both criticised and tested in authentic contexts. The linguistic matrix provided by the interplay between phases 1 and 2 is further refined in Phase 3 by target group, competitor and industry analysis and this information is duly fed into Phase 4 in its market share, cost structure and investment and finance account. These provide three basic calculations: profit and loss account, cash flow forecast and balance sheet. In Phase 5 the calculations are evaluated as objective ratios, as individual subjective heuristic evaluation and also as the interplay between the heuristic evaluation and the calculations through optimization techniques. Moreover, it is easy to integrate external expertise into this phase. Since the language of the model is English and it is an Internet-based solution these experts can be wherever needed. In the Phase 3 transformation process the match of customers' preferences and products characteristics is evaluated on the Likert scale. Then, employing soft computing and fuzzy logic, results can be produced. The competitor analysis is performed accordingly for each competitor and the capabilities of fulfilling customer groups' preferences can now be compared in an industry analysis. These analyses give the starting points for the defining phenomena of Phase 4, but they also give us some insights into the novelty level of the business idea. If our own product can fulfil customers' preferences when competitors cannot, we can say that the 'client' is unknown, that is, we can reach a higher level of novelty when it comes to this dimension. Two other factors of novelty (goal and path) are given by the phenomena of Phase 4. The nature of market share defines the 'goal'. If market share is expected to result from new markets where there are no competitors, we can say that the goal is unknown and the novelty level higher. The answer to "how to do that" (path) is given by cost structure and investments. Thus, it is possible to ensure that the idea innovated is still evaluated and developed as novel and innovative as it was in Phase 1 or whether it involves more or less potential as a novel idea.

From Five-Phase Model to Dynamics, Theories and Two-Layered Interplay Between Learning and Computing

Combining these findings the five-phased model is based on different theories and their exploitation. Innovation and development require different theories from the evaluation of existing business ideas. The interplay of Phases 1 and 2 creates an input for Phase 3. Phase 3 transforms the information so that it can be employed in Phase 4. Phase 4 produces the numerical information to be evaluated in Phase 5 through the subjective preferences and abilities defined in Phases 1 and 2. Phase 5 either produces the information required for the implementation of the idea or returns the learner to phase 1, 2 or 3. These theories and dynamics are summed up in Fig. 2.

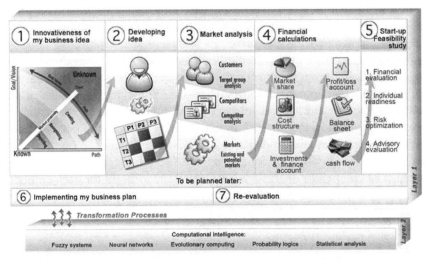

Fig. 2 Phases and theories that make up a business planning process

The starting point of this new modelling of business planning is a holistic, creative and innovative idea of the human being that emphasises the complex and complicate nature of human action. This means that complicated calculations, decision-making rules and large amount of numerical data cannot directly be presented to the learner as a meaningful construct. Therefore, technical solutions have to be differentiated from the learner's conceptual understanding into two layers and their transformation processes (see Fig. 2). This is solved by applying intelligent soft computing. Modelling humanlike intelligence in a computer environment has been problematic. Models of quantitative research have proven to be rather complicated, whereas in qualitative research computer modelling as such causes problems. The latest developments in intelligent soft computing, however, on the one hand facilitate more complex and complicated modelling of human logic and on the other transform its solutions into simple linguistic descriptions and interpretations (Zadeh 1996, 1997; Niskanen

1998). Integrating these opportunities as a two-layer construction provides the learner with an interface that is understandable (Layer 1) unlike the processes producing it (Layer 2). In this construct we can also collect quantitative and qualitative data if these are available, and then apply fuzzy linguistic cognitive maps (Axelrod 1976). Now in our modelling we mainly apply fuzzy reasoning, neural networks, evolutionary computing, probabilistic reasoning and statistical methods. Finally, we simulate and adjust our models according to empirical data and human expertise. The webpage as the learner's conceptual representation is simple and illustrative to work with while all the complicated modelling is built in java. This interplay offers on-line feedback to the learner who can then adjust and re-evaluate his/her ideas.

Summarising the Advancements of Modelling

Construction of the learning business plan model started with defining the meta-level approach and methodological basis for the research. This led to a five-phase model combining different phases with different theories with respect to holistic human nature. Integration of soft computing and learning environment created a two-layered approach to solving the transformation processes of complex information. These advances are summarized in Table 2.

Table 2 The advances in the learning business plan modelling process

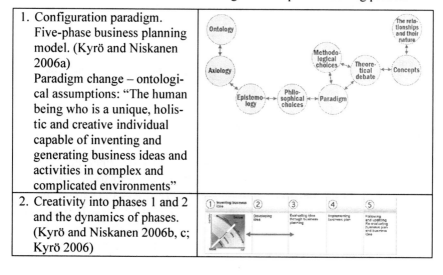

| 1. Configuration paradigm. Five-phase business planning model. (Kyrö and Niskanen 2006a) Paradigm change – ontological assumptions: "The human being who is a unique, holistic and creative individual capable of inventing and generating business ideas and activities in complex and complicated environments" | |
| 2. Creativity into phases 1 and 2 and the dynamics of phases. (Kyrö and Niskanen 2006b, c; Kyrö 2006) | |

3. Solution for phase 3 by using concept mapping. (Kyrö et al. 2006)	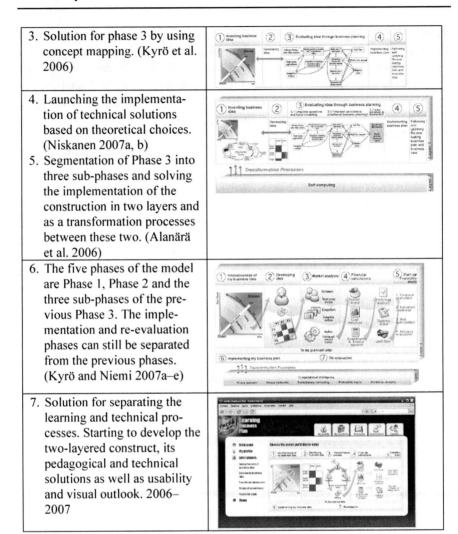
4. Launching the implementation of technical solutions based on theoretical choices. (Niskanen 2007a, b) 5. Segmentation of Phase 3 into three sub-phases and solving the implementation of the construction in two layers and as a transformation processes between these two. (Alanärä et al. 2006)	
6. The five phases of the model are Phase 1, Phase 2 and the three sub-phases of the previous Phase 3. The implementation and re-evaluation phases can still be separated from the previous phases. (Kyrö and Niemi 2007a–e)	
7. Solution for separating the learning and technical processes. Starting to develop the two-layered construct, its pedagogical and technical solutions as well as usability and visual outlook. 2006–2007	

Conclusions and Further Developments

Returning to the three problems of traditional business planning we have now tried to overcome all their essential aspects in order to provide a new business plan modelling that simultaneously considers the modelling and learning aspects of business planning. This modelling regards the human actor and his/her innovative action as a starting point and combines his/her abilities, resources and readiness into a context bound learning process. We have also broken the rules of linear and rational logic by applying concept maps and neuro-fuzzy reasoning that allow non-linear and more complex modelling. Mindful of Hindle's criticism, we have applied a reasonably consistent body of theoretical justification for developing and evaluating the business idea and defined the dynamics between different phases of this process. At the moment we are programming the interface between two layers with java and further developing the transformation and evaluation processes. To succeed in these two is, of course, a prerequisite for testing this modelling. On the other hand testing is needed for further adjusting the chosen concepts, decision-making rules and technical solutions. We hope this phase will take place next autumn. By using a problem-solving-oriented constructive research approach, we have succeeded in modelling business planning in a way that specifies its different phases and the dynamics between them. The five-phase model provides a learner-friendly two-layer solution for the complicated problems involved, and opens up a path for us to proceed with its practical simulation programming. This modelling has encouraged us to believe that it is possible to increase and teach creativeness in business planning and consequently help students to learn it and this way get also other benefits from business planning besides attracting equity investors. Perhaps this modelling allows us in future also increase our innovative abilities via business planning that is advancing business planning from planning to entrepreneurial learning.

References

Åhlberg M (1990) Käsitekarttatekniikka ja muuta vastaavat graafiset tiedonesittämistekniikat opettajan ja oppilaiden työvälineinä. University of Joensuu. Kasvatustieteiden tiedekunnan tutkimuksia No 30

Åhlberg M (1993) Concept maps, vee diagrams and rhetorical argumentation (ra) analysis: three educational theory-based tools to facilitate meaningful learning. Paper Presented at the Third International Seminar on Misconceptions in Science and Mathematics. August 1–5, 1993. Cornell University. Published electronically in the Proceedings of the Seminar

Åhlberg M (2001) Käsitekartat tutkimusmenetelmänä. In Valli, R. & Aaltonen, J. (toim.) Ikkunoita tutkimusmetodeihin I. (in press)

Alanärä M (2004) Comparative analysis of business planning literature Unpublished report. University of Tampere

Alanärä M, Kyrö P, Niemi M, Somersalmi V (2006) New Generation Business Planning. Paper Presented at the BEPART 2006 Conference

Axelrod R (1976) Structure of Decision, the Cognitive Maps of Political Elites. Princeton University Press, Princeton

Carrier C (2005) Pedagogical challenges in entrepreneurship education. The dynamics of learning entrepreneurship in a cross-cultural university context, P. Kyrö and C. Carrier, Entrepreneurship Education Series 2/2005, Hämeenlinna: University of Tampere, Research Centre for Vocational and Professional Education

Carter NM, Gartner WB, Reinolds PD (1996) Exploring start-up event sequences. Journal of Business Venturing, 11:151–166

Davidsson P, Delmar F, Wiklund J (2002) Entrepreneurship as growth; growth as entrepreneurship, in Hilt MA, Ireland RD, Camp, SM, Sexton DL (Eds.) Strategic Entrepreneurship, Blackwell, Cambridge

Delmar F, Shane S (2004) Legimitating first: organizing activities and the survival of new ventures. Journal of Business Venturing, 19:385–410

DeTienne DR, Chandler GN (2004) Opportunity identification and its role in the entrepreneurial classroom: a pedagogical approach and empirical test. Academy of Management Learning and Education, 3(3):242–257

Drucker P (1959) Long-range planning challenge to management science, Management Science. Journal of the Institute of Management Sciences (April):238–249

Eijnatten FM (2005) A chaordic lens for understanding entrepreneurship and intrapreneurship, in Fayolle A, Kyrö P, Uljin J (Eds.) Entrepreneurship Research in Europe: Perspectives and Outcomes, Edward Elgar, Cheltenham

Fiet JO (2001) The pedagogical side of entrepreneurship theory. Journal of Business Venturing, 16(2):101–117

Hindle K (1997) An Enhanced Paradigm of Entrepreneurial Business Planning. Swinburne University of Technology, Swinburne

Jones MV, Dimitratos P (2003) Editorial introduction: creativity, process, and time: the antithesis of "Instant International". Journal of International Entrepreneurship, 1(2):159–162

Karlsson T (2005) Business Plans in New Ventures – An institutional perspective. JIBS Dissertation series No. 030. Jönköping International Business School

Kyrö P (2007) A Theoretical Framework for Planning: Conducting and Evaluating Entrepreneurship Education. Presented at the EFMD 36th EISB Conference 6–8 September 2006, Southampton, United Kingdom

Kyrö P, Niemi M (2007a) Uusia avauksia liiketoimintasuunnitelman opettamiseen. Article published in Yrittäjyyskasvatuksen monia suuntia – book by Lehtonen Heleena, Kyrö Paula and Ristimäki Kari, publication series of the School of Economics and Business Administration of University of Tampere 2007

Kyrö P, Niemi M (2007b) Liiketoimintasuunnitelman laatimisesta – innovatiiviseen mallintamiseen. Paper presented at Yrittäjyystutkimuspäivät, Vaasa 2007

Kyrö P, Niemi M (2007c) Advancing Teaching and Learning Business Planning, Paper Presented at the ICSB2007 World Conference in Turku, June 2007

Kyrö P, Niemi M (2007d) Innovative Modelling for Learning Business Planning, Paper presented at the IntEnt2007 Conference in Poland, July 2007

Kyrö P, Niemi M (2007e) An Application for Learning Business Planning, Paper to be Presented at the EFMD2007 Conference in Slovenia, autumn 2007

Kyrö, P, Niemi, M, Somersalmi V (2006) Teaching Business Planning – Art or Science, Paper Presented at the ESU2006 Conference on summer 2006

Kyrö P, Niskanen VA (2006a) A Novel Proactive Meta-Level Approach to Configuration of Soft-Computing Modelling, Paper Presented at the IPMU Conference

Kyrö P, Niskanen VA (2006b) Innovativeness and a need for new configuration and modelling for Business planning. Paper presented at the 6th European Summer University 2006. Entrepreneurship in Europe, Entrepreneurship & Sustainability June 29–July 5, 2006 Dauphine University, Paris, France

Kyrö P, Niskanen VA (2006C) Modelling Innovativeness and Creativity in Business Planning. Paper Presented at the KES2006 Conference, Bournemouth International Conference Centre 9th, 10th and 11th of October

Lukk (2001) "The Constructive Research Approach." http://www.metodix.com

Menzies TV (2005) Entrepreneurship Education at Universities Across Canada. The dynamics of learning entrepreneurship in a cross-cultural university context, P. Kyrö and C. Carrier (2005), Entrepreneurship Education Series 2/2005, Hämeenlinna: University of Tampere, Research Centre for Vocational and Professional Education

Niskanen VA (1998) Soft Computing Methods in Human Sciences, Faciliative Tools in Schools and Corporations, Springer, Heidelberg, Lawrence Erlbaum Associates, Mahwah, New Jersey

Niskanen V (2007a) Business Planning Evaluation with Soft Computing. Paper Presented at the FUZZIEEE07 Conference

Niskanen V (2007b) Application of Fuzzy Cognitive Maps to Business Planning Models. Paper presented at the IFSA Conference

Puhakka V (2002) Entrepreneurial business opportunity recognition: Relationships between intellectual and social capital, environmental dynamism, opportunity recognition behavior, and performance. Business Administration 42. Management and Organization

Robinson RB (1979) Forecasting and small business: a study of the strategic planning process. Journal of Small Business Management, 17:19–27

Saks NT, Gaglio CM (2002) Can opportunity identification be taught? Journal of Enterprising Culture, 10(4):313–334

Sarasvathy SD (2001a) Causation and effectuation: toward a theoretical shift from economic inevitability to entrepreneurial contingency. Academy of Management Review, 26(2):243–288

Sarasvathy S.D (2001b) Effectual reasoning in entrepreneurial decision making: Existence and bounds, Winner of the Newman Award at the 2001 Academy of Management Meeting in Washington DC

Timmons J (1994) New Venture Creation, Entrepreneurship for the Twenty-First Century. 4th edition. Irwin, Illinois

Yiu L, Briggs J (2000) Conference on Chaos Theory and the Arts in the Context of Social, Economic and Organizational Development, Geneva: Centre for Socio-Economic Development

Zadeh L (1996) Fuzzy Logic = Computing with words. IEEE Transactions on Fuzzy Systems, 2:103–111

Zadeh L (1997) Toward a theory of fuzzy information granulation and its centrality in human reasoning and fuzzy logic. Fuzzy Sets and Systems, 90(2):111–127

Entrepreneurship Education in Context: A Case Study of the University of Twente

P. van der Sijde[*] and A. Ridder

University of Twente, Enschede, The Netherlands

Introduction

The University of Twente is an entrepreneurial university; this means more than just having a focus on entrepreneurship, but in the framework of this paper we restrict ourselves to this (for a more elaborate discussion on the entrepreneurial university we refer to Shane 2004; Clark 1998; Bok 2003). Entrepreneurship is an essential and consistent element in the university policy since the early 1980s and concerns infrastructure, spin-offs, teaching and research. In this paper we first give an overview of the context and how it evolved in Twente, then we focus on the teaching programme and we close with some remarks.

Entrepreneurship in Context

At the beginning of the 1980s entrepreneurship as a university issue started to take shape in the region of Twente in The Netherlands. In 1982 the incubator BTC (Business and Technology Centre)-Twente opened its doors for companies and especially young companies originating from the university. In the BTC-Twente companies could hire flexible office and production space, which would enable them to 'grow' with their markets. The BTC-Twente today still is an important component of the knowledge infrastructure for entrepreneurship in Twente. In 1984 the University of Twente established its start-up programme TOP (temporary entrepreneurial positions). The TOP programme enabled graduates (and other enterprising persons) to start a company with the support of the university. The support consisted (and still does) of an interest free loan, office space,

P.C. van der Sijde et al. (eds.), *Teaching Entrepreneurship.*
© Physica-Verlag Berlin Heidelberg 2008

access to university networks and training, for the period of 1 year. Since 1984 the university has been instrumental in the establishment of some 500 companies via this programme. Also around 1984 an elective training course was developed by the School of Technology and Management (as it was called at that time): "Become your own Boss". In this course the students were taught how to write and present a business plan.

These three elements (BTC-Twente, TOP, and "Become your own Boss") and the business network for the pioneering university start-ups that the UT co-initiated in 1989, are the cornerstones for the further development of the Twente entrepreneurship structure. Since then many new building blocks were added (see also Fig. 1). Parallel to these developments, the UT has adapted its internal structures and procedures to facilitate its entrepreneurial activities. In the mid-1980s for example the School of Technology and Management founded a centre for entrepreneurship, which developed into the Dutch Institute for Knowledge-intensive Entrepreneurship "Nikos" in 2002.

Development of the Infrastructure

The BTC-Twente was the first visible institute on what later became the Business & Science Park (B&SP) Twente; a park of over 40 ha (100 acres) located next to the University. Over the years it developed and many small companies and a couple of larger companies took tenancy at the park. A recent development is the Kennispark ("Knowledge Park"), which extends the B&SP Twente and includes (part) of the university campus and an adjacent area designated to house high-tech companies. At the university campus special facilities are established for high-tech companies in the areas of nano-microtechnology, biomedical technology and IT.

Stimulating Entrepreneurship

The TOP programme is the basis for other initiatives to stimulate entrepreneurship. In the mid-1990s the Student Union, a then newly formed body for the promotion of the students' interests, together with the TOP management, developed a version for student-entrepreneurs – University Student Enterprises (USE). Students are supported via training, networks, and (office) facilities. TOP also became one of the pillars under the project

"Successfully your own Boss". This project has a second pillar that helps aspiring entrepreneurs without a business idea to find this and establish a company (within a period of 6 months). The project focuses not on specific groups; nevertheless one group is unemployed people. This also is a successful project in which about 70% of the participants become economically active (most of them start a company, a few find a job). This approach is currently being translated into the Venture Lab Twente, a programme for high-tech and high-potentials. Inside the university an entrepreneurial climate has been worked on, through the participation of researchers, Ph.D.'s and executive staff in tailor made courses.

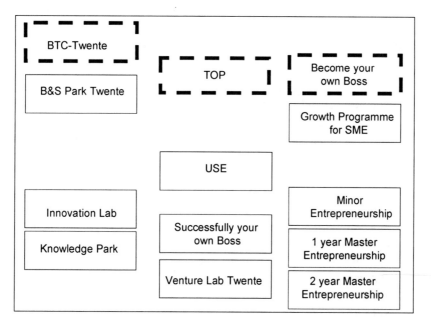

Fig. 1 Building blocks of the Twente structure for entrepreneurship

Entrepreneurship Courses

The course "Become your own Boss" has been for many years the only course on entrepreneurship at the university. At the end of the 1980s a second course was developed. Although this course was primarily developed for owner-managers of companies, who were preparing the next stage of their companies, the course was set up in such a manner, that students supported the entrepreneurs to do the 'leg work' (finding information, writing sections of the business plan). Via this course that is called "Growth Programme" for the entrepreneurs, the students got an insight into the boardrooms of SMEs. This was the entrepreneurship teaching situation by the mid-1990s.

Teaching Entrepreneurship: The Minor Programme

The teaching of entrepreneurship really got started in 1999; the year the Minor Entrepreneurship started. The target group for this programme are all students of the university in their third year; in their third year the students have to choose a "minor" – the Minor Entrepreneurship is one of those. The programme (total 20 EC) has gone already through many changes; at present it consists of three fixed and two optional courses:

- *Market-oriented entrepreneurship*: The central issue in this course is opportunity recognition and marketing. The students learn the basics of marketing and prepare a marketing plan either for their own company or for an entrepreneur.
- *Financial management in SMEs*: The financial aspects of starting and running a company are the topic in this course (balance sheets, the connection between strategy and finance, sources of finance).
- *Legal aspects of SMEs*: All legal aspects of a company are the topic in this course.
- *Become your own boss*: The students learn to write a business plan for a company they want to start, or recently started, or for an entrepreneur. The students either have to do this course, or do the course.
- *Supporting an entrepreneur in the growth programme*: The students provide consultancy and hands-on support for an entrepreneur who writes a new business plan for his company.

After some time we also developed a variant for business students. Since these students already had basic knowledge on marketing and legal issues they were originally excluded from the Minor Entrepreneurship programme. However, many of them became interested in this minor programme when we explained the differences between managing an existing business and starting a business. In stead of "Market-oriented Entrepreneurship" we offer business students "High-tech Marketing". In this course the students have to write a marketing plan for a (new) technology or a high-tech product. In stead of "Legal aspects of SMEs" a course on "Knowledge Development and Protection" is offered. The Minor for the business students is a variant of the original Minor; in due time this variant will be developed into a new Minor program focusing on entrepreneurship and com-mercialization of services. The Minor Entrepreneurship also functions as a 'bridge' for students who want to do the Business Administration Master track "Innovation and Entrepreneurship" but do not have a sufficiently matching bachelor degree.

Entrepreneurship Concept in the Minor

The entrepreneurship concept used to develop the Minor programme is rooted in the Entrepreneurship in Networks (EiN) model developed in Nikos. This model combines two strands of theory: the process approach to entrepreneurship (e.g. Van der Veen and Wakkee 2004) and a social systems approach (Groen 2005) – see Fig. 2.

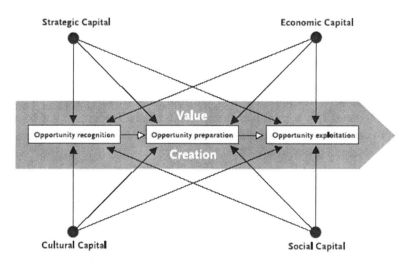

Fig. 2 Entrepreneurship in networks model

In the process approach to entrepreneurship, the process starts with an idea that needs to be developed into an opportunity, which means business (this is a topic in Market-oriented Entrepreneurship), a business plan is an important stage/tool in this process. A business plan defines what is needed to bring the opportunity to 'life' into exploitation, indicating the resources that are needed. All courses contribute to the "cultural capital" of the student (knowledge on entrepreneurship and entrepreneurial processes). "Strategic capital" (strategic issues) is one of the topics in Financial Management as well as in Market-oriented Entrepreneurship. The "economic capital" is primarily discussed in Financial Management in SMEs, while the "social capital" (networks) are dealt with in the practical courses "Become your own Boss" and the "Growth Programme". Of course the students learn about enterprise, but primarily through and for enterprise. Kolb's learning cycle is applied: theory is provided in the classroom, practice is provided in the 'field' (working with enterprises), and reflection is stimulated via assignments.

Teaching Entrepreneurship: The Master Programme

The Master Programme at first was completely dedicated to Entrepreneurship. Since 2007 the programme is part of the Business Administration Master and focuses on Innovation and Entrepreneurship (INN&ENT). The University of Twente has chosen for a broad Master programme in Business Administration (M.Sc. Programme). In this programme four courses are the same for all students and there are two track-specific courses. These two courses (each 5 EC) are:

- *Business development in networks*: In this course students learn about business development and the role of networks in this process. This course has a practical component where students have to screen a company with regards to their networks and/or their business development processes.
- *Principles of entrepreneurship*: The students learn about the historic development of the field, trends and emerging issues. They have to do a group assignment (mostly practice related) and an individual assignment (write a paper).

There also is a 2 year Master programme, although not officially at the University of Twente. The Aalborg University in Denmark offers a 2 year Master programme and as the Twente and the Aalborg curricula are complementary we explored the joint offer of a 2 year programme. In this programme students from Aalborg and Twente do their first semesters (first half year starting in September) at their home universities. The second semester (starting in February), the students do the programme in Aalborg where the emphasis in this particular phase is on regional innovation systems and entrepreneurship. The third semester (September, second year), the courses take place at the University of Twente and focus on high-tech entrepreneurship (e.g. high-tech marketing, protection of knowledge); the final part of the programme, the thesis work, can be done at either university, but under joint supervision.

Entrepreneurship Concept the Master

Like in the Minor programme, the Master courses are designed using the EiN model. The process, as well as the capitals, are modelled in the courses. Different from the Minor programme, the focus in the Master track is rather on applying the principle "about enterprise" and to a lesser degree on "through enterprise".

Teaching Entrepreneurship in Other Curricula

Gradually the technical sciences bachelor programmes acknowledge that entrepreneurial knowledge and skills are a 'must' to prepare students for their future careers. Second year "Industrial Design" bachelors are made aware of the relevance of making marketing and financial plans when designing new products, and the possibilities of such products as the basis of a new company. Of course this then requires a business plan. The minor course "Market-oriented Entrepreneurship" is compulsive in their curriculum and a growing number of these students take the "Financial Management in SMEs" course as an elective. Bachelors in "Advanced Technologies" are introduced to entrepreneurship through compulsory courses "Innovation and Entrepreneurship", in their first and second year. In the second year they complete their entrepreneurship training when they enter -in groups- into a business plan competition. The ideas for the business plans are supplied by researchers of science and technology. The students present their plans to a jury of professionals e.g. from incubators, banks and regional support agencies and they can win a prize. As of 2009, a Technology Venturing course will be offered to students in the Master Nanotechnology.

Teaching Entrepreneurship: Extracurricular Programmes

Nikos is involved in two extracurricular courses. The first one is designed for pupils of the fifth grade of secondary schools (17 years of age) and is an introduction to entrepreneurship. This course is built upon three pillars: theory, practice and research. The course consists of eight afternoons and all follow the same format: first part is 'theory', than 'practice' and finally some research in the domain is presented. At the end of the course the pupils present a business plan on a poster. The course has been prepared and will first be taught in 2009. Basically the Entrepreneurship Adventure, designed for bachelor and master students of all studies, but extracurricular and organized by the Student Union as part of the Skills Certificate project, is similar. In these extracurricular courses also a process approach is used and each of the four capitals is dealt with. Further, both courses can be characterized as "for enterprise".

Teaching Entrepreneurship

At the University of Twente teaching is an important element in the knowledge infrastructure for entrepreneurship; it was also the last element to reach the stage of maturity. Could it have been different? Could the structure only have contained a teaching programme without the rest? In Twente the development at the university was from 'outside' in: first there was the incubator, and then the spin-off programme followed by an elective course. The teaching programme matured after the maturation of the infrastructure (incubators and spin-off support) and it moved from being extracurricular toward curricular. Following maturity, a next step, presently at the very early stages of preparation, might be targeted entrepreneurship support for women and female researchers in the high-tech areas.

Nowadays there is a university wide support for entrepreneurship in general and spin-offs (commercialization of knowledge and technology) in particular. Schools, other than the School of Management and Governance, implement entrepreneurship – together with Nikos. This enables Nikos not only to teach, but also to carry out an extensive research programme on entrepreneurship. The philosophy of Nikos is that you can only teach entrepreneurship, when you are also involved in putting entrepreneurship in practice (e.g. being involved in spin-off and start-up programmes), and in research. Theory and practice should cross fertilize each other – for the benefit of teaching as well as to further entrepreneurship as a scientific discipline.

References

Bok D (2003) Universities in the marketplace. Princeton: Princeton University Press

Clark B (1998) Creating entrepreneurial universities. Oxford: Pergamon

Groen AJ (2005) Knowledge intensive entrepreneurship in networks: towards a multi-level, multi-dimensional approach. Journal of Enterprising Culture, 13(1): 69–88

Shane S (2004) Academic entrepreneurship. University spinoffs and wealth crea-
    tion. Cheltenham: Edward Elgar
Veen M van der, Wakkee I (2004) Understanding the entrepreneurial process,
    Arpent, Vol. 2, pp. 114–152, Brussels: European Foundation for Management
    Development

Entrepreneurship Training by Action Learning in a University Context: The Case of ROXI

C. Diensberg

HIE-RO, University of Rostock, Rostock, Germany

Introduction: Origins and Institutional Setting of ROXI

This case illustrates the origin, implementation and Action Learning approach of the entrepreneurship support programme ROXI (acronym for 'Rostocker Existenzgründer Initiative'). ROXI is administered by the Hanseatic Institute for Entrepreneurship and Regional Development (HIE-RO) at the University of Rostock in North-East Germany. ROXI offers extra-curricular, supplementary training and support opportunities for students, graduates and university staff (cf. also Braun et al. 1998). Starting out as a mere training concept, the programme expanded its activities over the years to include pre-incubating work (e.g. sensitizing, motivating, informing), and into the start-up phase (e.g. coaching, consulting). The initiative for ROXI had already taken off in 1996 at the newly established Chair for Economics and Business Education of the University. Interviewed for this case, one of the originators tells:

> *"Major reasons to develop ROXI were the high regional unemployment rates and low economic growth at the time. Germany's reunification in 1990 and the transformation from a socialist central planning system into a market economy did not only bring new freedom to Eastern Germany, but also meant a collapse of a sudden, non-competitive industry. We believed that our university and our chair had potential to become active for counter-actions. And we thought that an entrepreneurship training programme could be effective as a long-term-approach for regional growth and to fight unemployment. Our role models were entrepreneurship training programmes in developing and threshold countries, rather than university programmes. When we started to promote the idea for ROXI, such activities were still uncommon within a German university. Rostock was insofar no exception, but rather the rule."*

P.C. van der Sijde et al. (eds.), *Teaching Entrepreneurship.*
© Physica-Verlag Berlin Heidelberg 2008

Towards implementation, one of the first steps was to organize wider idea support. Selected University faculty, regional business people and administration officials were addressed to support and promote the plan. Approval to fast-track implementation by establishing an independent but university-attached institute was given by a government official. The foundation HIE-RO (previously known as "Institute for HRD at the University of Rostock") in 1997 created the platform for the entrepreneurship training. The above quoted co-founder recollects today:

"From our point of view, this new setting promised some advantages to the alternative of integrating the training into university curricula:

- *We could save time. The entrepreneurship training could take off quickly.*
- *Some distance to traditional academic teaching gave us more freedom for a clear focus on application and on Action Learning. It also promised better conditions for programme development. Such a programme was new for us; an experiment so to speak.*
- *With an attached institute we could also keep the strong university relation. We could build laboratory conditions for Action Learning and entrepreneurship education, and keep them linked to our chair and university work.*
- *Openness and flexibility promised more than an integrated course could offer, for example in terms of selecting participants, contracting trainers, amending course content and methods, or in allowing changes of staff.*
- *A major reason for building a new institute was, at the beginning, funding. Formal requirements of the foreseeable options did not allow direct university funding."*

Since 1997, the main financing for ROXI is provided by the federal German state of Mecklenburg-Vorpommern (grants of the State Ministry of Labour and Economy, co-financed by the European Social Fund). This funding background is one of the reasons why the number of created start-ups and new jobs are important success indicators by which ROXI is evaluated. "You must know that our funding needs to be re-applied for on a 2-year-basis." The University of Rostock provides the working space and rooms for ROXI.

Outline of the Training

Target groups for the trainings by ROXI are students, graduates, study drop-outs and university staff with a willingness to develop a business idea. Heterogeneity is desired, and professional or study backgrounds don't matter. Marketing for the training is done throughout the university and partly beyond, by means of mailings, recommendations by faculty or former participants, leaflets, and informative events. Without a 'roadshow', the training would not find its target group (as participation is voluntary). In addition sensitizing and motivational effects for entrepreneurship would then be much lower than desired, and the entrepreneurial potentials of the University would be less visible, too.

The full training course has a duration of 120 training hours and runs four times a year. During the two seme ster breaks, it is offered daily over 3 weeks. Parallel to semesters, the trai ning takes place on Friday afternoons and full-time on Saturdays. While regular university courses are free of charge in Germany, ROXI asks for a participant fee of € 100 for the full training course.

"Hereby we aim to support commitment for the course-work and to keep free-riders out. Two experimental attempts with courses for free did indeed show higher drop-out rates and negative effects in terms of participant cohesion and learning dynamics."

Before entering the training, interested participants attend an interview with the project manager-in-charge. This obligatory 'match meeting' aims to matching mutual expectations. For example, potential participants often want to know if the training promises real support, why regular attendance is expected, or what the work load entails. Vice versa, the project manager wants to know if the training is suitable for the potential entrepreneur with his or her basic business idea. Normally, each training course attracts between 7 and 12 participants.

The training ends with a presentation and oral defence of the business plans in front of a panel of external experts. Participants also get a certificate issued by the institute; participation is not accredited for bachelor, master or diploma courses of the University. Those participants who enter into business start-up immediately after the course (on average 50%) may use further coaching and consultancy support by ROXI or by other providers.

"Additional services like coaching and consulting did not initially belong to our ideas. When we started ROXI we assumed that participants would help themselves after course completion and would have learned to fly as full fledged entrepreneurs. It may be that this was a bit naïve. We had to learn that a mere course offering is not sufficient to meet the demand. Entrepreneurship is a learning process for which we shouldn't dictate a full stop after three weeks training. Many participants expect us to offer additional support into their start up phase. We also thought, in the beginning, that we would attract many more 'high potentials', in terms of high tech, in terms of market potential, and in terms of entrepreneurial personalities. But our experience over the years is that we attract all kinds of business ideas - chiefly services. Pure high tech ideas are an exception, and most

of the participants are 'normal performers'. To put it bluntly: The real 'high potentials' start up with or without all these entrepreneurship programmes. They don't want to loose time in a three weeks course but prefer short seminars, consultancy services and capital access. Vice versa, 'low potentials' avoid intense training courses and preparation. This is what we also had to learn over the years. However, we are obviously attractive to a wide range of potential entrepreneurs. These people are surprisingly normal, in all their different facets and personalities, with their different business ideas and, off course, their different hopes and dreams."

An empirical survey in 2003 among students at the University of Rostock affirmed the programmes' popularity – 87% of the students were aware of the courses offered by ROXI and the project itself (Wilde 2005). Figure 1 (next page) shows the conceptual base of the training. The corresponding training plan (see Table 1 – 2 pages onward) arranges topics and times for each day of the 3 weeks full course during semester breaks. The final panel presentation of business plans follows normally with a distance of up to 2 weeks. (Marked fields in the table refer to the exemplified Action Learning exercises within the final paragraph of this case).

ROXI cooperates with experts from different professional backgrounds as trainers. Each course involves 10–15 facilitators, mainly recruited from the business sector and honorary-contracted. However, the project manager is the main contact person for the participants, with a regular presence as co-trainer or supervisor; this aims at continuity. Performance of the external trainers is constantly observed and evaluated by course participants and project manager-in-charge. Results are utilized for change decisions. It took some years until a basic trainer pool could be established, and this work continues today. First steps towards a 'train-the-trainer' programme have been taken.

The Action Learning Approach Used by ROXI: Conceptual Background

As one ROXI trainer states:

"We should not simply ask if entrepreneurship is taught in a University but rather how learning is supported. A wrong teaching for entrepreneurship may even harm, like wrong medical treatment can harm healing."

The pedagogical approach by ROXI is based on Action Learning. But what does Action Learning really mean? Literature and other sources show different understandings of a not clearly defined term. One will regularly find the name of Revans (1980) as one renowned originator. Indeed, the ROXI approach for Action Learning can be linked to such ideas, but it has quite other origins and references. Role models for ROXI were entrepreneurship training programmes in developing and threshold countries, of which the most influential one for ROXI was the programme CEFE (Competency based Economies through Formation of Enterprise). CEFE started

Post-Training Phase: Consulting/Coaching into Start-up (on demand)		
Fine-Tuning the Business Plan; Viability Test	*Finalizing and optimizing the Business Plan. Preparing a BP-presentation. Presenting the BP in front of a panel of external experts.*	Presentation of the Business Plan
Finance	*Capital budgeting. Cost planning. Break Even analysis. Cash Flow analysis. Balance Sheet/Profit and loss account. Return on Investment. Financial planning.*	Formulation of the Business Plan
Organization, Management, Law and Legal Matters	*Selection of an appropriate business model and the legal form for my business. Organization and optimization of my business processes. Employee management.*	
Product Development, Production Planning, Technology	*Evaluating the aspects of my product or service in terms of their value for the customers. Organization of an efficient production process, the logistics and identification of my relevant suppliers.*	
Marketing, Competition	*Identification of my customers and their needs, my competitors and my market segment or niche. Chances of improvement, useful marketing strategies.*	
SWOT-Analysis of the Business Ideas	*Estimation of strengths, weaknesses, opportunities and threats for my business idea. Deduction of promising action strategies from the SWOT-analysis.*	Matching the would-be entrepreneur and business project
Idea Development, Idea Screening and Evaluation	*Development and evaluation of new ideas. Context to supports me in the idea development. Development of my creativity potential. Valuation of my priorities for idea implementation. Combination of idea development with goal setting and follow-up management.*	Developing basic entrepreneurial competences
External Environment, Branch Situation	*Basic global and general trends. Meeting certain branch expectations with my professional background. Data mining in terms of branch-relevant information. Knowledge about "How to play the game?"*	
Risk Behaviour, Management Competences	*Dealing with and managing risks. Decision making on limited information. Development of leadership competence. Difference btw. management and leadership. Organization of teams. Essentials of good planning? Skills in selling and negotiating.*	
Motivation, Goal-Setting, Networking, Determination/Stamina	*Definition of my relevant goals. Settlement of achievable goals. Recognition of the things of personal attraction and interest, of my preferred working environment and of the ability of inspiring others. Networking.*	
Pre-Training Phase: Match-Meeting, Pre-Support (e.g. for a basic business idea to work with)		

Fig. 1 Conceptual base of the ROXI training. Source: ROXI Training Material, HIE-RO, Spring 2007

Table 1 Course content of the training

Time	Monday	Tuesday	Wednesday	Thursday	Friday
First week					
09.00–10.30	Welcome, expectations, rules	Entrepreneurial competences (goal-setting)	Entrepreneurial competences (dealing with risks)	Environment (information resources)	Environment (application to the own BP)
10.45–12.30	Getting to know each other	Entrepreneurial competences (networking, negotiating)	Entrepreneurial competences (customer-orientation)	Environment (trends, business models, rules of the game)	Idea development & refinement (creativity techniques)
13.15–14.45	Entrepreneurial competences (overview)	Entrepreneurial competences (management, leadership)	Entrepreneurial competences (self-perception, resources/personal SWOT)	Environment (application/ out of class exercise)	Idea development & refinement (innovating, optimizing)
15.00–17.00	Entrepreneurial competences (motivation)	Entrepreneurial competences (team building)	Environment (entrepreneurship support structures)	Environment (application/ out of class exercise)	Idea development & refinement (innovating, optimizing)
Homework			*Customer contacts*	*Investigations*	*Innovation of idea*
Second week					
09.00–10.30	Idea development and refinement (personal values/criteria)	Marketing (introduction; customer behaviour)	Marketing (branch specifics)	Marketing (market research)	Production planning (project planning, costs)
10.45–12.30	Idea development and refinement (opportunity related criteria)	Marketing (structures, branch-specifics, pricing)	Marketing (international)	Business concept (revision of SWOT-analysis and business concept)	Production planning (costs, margin, break even)
13.15–14.45	Idea development and refinement (conceptual SWOT)	Marketing (proposing value)	Marketing (market research)	Marketing (individual marketing plan)	Production planning (value architecture, kaizen)
15.00–17.00	Business concept (conceptual SWOT; value proposition)	Marketing (case study)	Marketing (market research)	Business concept (risk analysis)	Production planning (individual plan)
Homework	*BP Chaps. 1 and ***2.2*	*Market research*	*Summary of market research*	*BP Chap. 2*	*Collection of data on costs*
Third week					
09.00–10.30	Production planning (individual plan)	Organisation and management (legal forms of enterprises)	Financial planning (book-keeping, tax statements)	Organisation and management (controlling, BSC)	Finishing the BP (layout/graphics)
10.45–12.30	Production planning (individual plan)	Organisation and management (contract law)	Financial planning (profit & loss statement, balance sheet, taxes)	Organisation & management (controlling, insolvency prevention)	Finishing the BP (layout/graphics)
13.15–14.45	Organisation and management (structures, communication)	Financial planning (cash flow, investment, profitability)	Financial planning (profit and loss statement, balance sheet, taxes)	Entrepreneurial competences (presentation techniques)	Course ending (evaluation/ feedback)
15.00–17.00	Organisation and management (conflicts and crises)	Financial planning (financing, credit, loan programmes)	Financial planning (individual plans)	Entrepreneurial competences (presentation techniques)	"Final rehearsal" for plan presentations
Homework	*BP, Chap. 3*	*BP, Chap. 4*	*BP, Chap. 4*	*BP Chap. 5*	*BP-presentation*

Source: ROXI Training Material, HIE-RO, Spring 2007

in the mid 1980s by the German Agency for Technical Cooperation (GTZ); programme founder was Rainer Kolshorn. The pedagogy of CEFE is strongly influenced by modern psychological and pedagogic concepts (e.g. the work of Jean Piaget) and by US-American entrepreneurship research (e.g. by findings of David C. McClelland or by Robert H. Brockhaus).

"The CEFE training approach is based on an experiential and action learning methodology. Games and exercises simulating the different fields of business environment and entrepreneurial functions, role plays, field work to collect the necessary data, the group dynamics of participants, and feed back from bankers are most important media of learning. (...) The learning impacts from such experiences and action are much more effective than from teaching and lecturing." (CEFE 2007)

Similarly, ROXI realizes Action Learning as learning:

- Which starts with and is based on real life and real problems.
- Which combines 'hands-on activities' and 'mental activities'.
- Which is an interactive and social activity, a learning with and from others.
- Which needs to query the situation as well as the actions of the learner.
- Which challenges constant interpretation and evaluation.
- Which leads to some kind of generalizing conclusions and improved competence.
- Which finally improves applications and deeper experience.

Figure 2 visualizes basic assumptions and consequences for the use of Action Learning within the HIE-RO/ROXI training course.

Our model first refers to the person (entrepreneur), to the business idea and to the environment as important success factors, according to entrepreneurship research. A traditional 'factor-understanding' is combined here with a modern 'systems-understanding'. Factors do not effect in a linear way, and cannot be separated from the entrepreneur as an open, actively constructing and self-regulating human being. The crucial matter is the mental model(ling) of the entrepreneur which the figure places into the centre. Mental modelling (perceiving, interpreting, valuing, mental interacting ...) is seen as core activity of the entrepreneur, together with the more visible and perceivable actions.

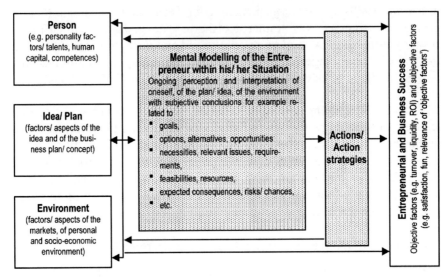

Fig. 2 Success model of Entrepreneurial Action. Source: adapted from Braun and Diensberg (2001, p. 61)

In accord with other entrepreneurship researchers, for example Göbel and Frese (1999) who state "only activities can lead to entrepreneurial success", our model highlights and integrates:

- Mental activities (modelling as acting to ones own inside, e.g. changing the ways to perceive and building resources to know).
- Outside effecting, visible and hands-on activities.

Action Learning activates both kinds of activities within learning and for achieving certain learning goals. It is more than mere activity inside or outside of a classroom.

As a consequence, ROXI is working with training exercises in a communicative and feed-back assuring group work which:

- Put the participants into a goal-oriented problem situation (e.g. of a marketing situation).
- Where they have to act and to find first or interim solutions.
- Which will be published to the group.
- Which will then be evaluated and interpreted together with the group.
- With the aim to work out general conclusions.

- Which can be applied in similar or a repeated situations (which means that also exercises are party repeated towards stepwise improved solutions and findings).
- And which can finally be applied and transferred onto the specific entrepreneurial project of the single participants.

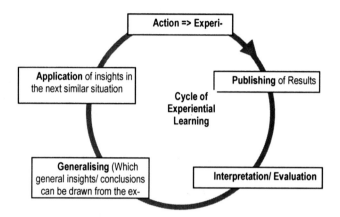

Fig. 3 The Cycle of Experiential Learning (based on Kolb 1984). Source: GTZ (2000)

The experiential learning environment (Fig. 3) which ROXI creates does not teach and impart knowledge in the traditional way of teaching in schools or universities. Rather, this environment provides:

- Structural conditions which provide problem situations as practical and relevant perceivable challenges, together with work objectives, needed resources (e.g. facts, information, work material, media), and support for effective group work.
- Roles of the trainers as facilitators (e.g. as providers of structures which are conducive to learning and questioning, as general process observers, as promoters of reflection and as feed-back givers, as co-players).
- Roles of the participants as active framers (constructers, producers) of their learning, of their competence development and of their knowledge transfer into their entrepreneurial activities (e.g. their own business model and plan).

Action Learning Exercises Used Within ROXI: Practice

'Introducing Each Other: My Life in Brief'

We are entering the second training session of the first day of the training, this time with seven participants. A course introduction had already been made, and the ROXI manager Mrs. Meier is the trainer today. Prepared material on the tables are old magazines, four scissors, four glue sticks, masking tape, crayons, and seven sheets of large flipchart paper.

> *"Welcome back from the break. Let us get to know each other better! The exercise which we will do next is simply called 'My Life in Brief', and you will be asked to make a collage and to depict your life with drawings, text and pictures. Where do I come from? What have I done so far? What are my ideas or dreams for my life and living? Where am I heading? What is my business idea? All the material which you can use is here on the table and you might need to share scissors or glue sticks. There is a sheet of flipchart paper for each of you; don't forget to write your name on it too. You will be given 15 min. to prepare the collage. Afterwards, each of you will be asked to present yourself and your goals to the group."*

Observing the participants, we notice most start with enthusiasm, while two seem reluctant. As one participant seizes a scissor and glue stick without wanting to share, he gives cause for a conflict; two other settle the difference. Concentrated individual work alternates with communication and other interaction until Mrs. Meier announces a remaining time of 2 min. – hectic activity breaks out. Mrs. Meier stops the work, though not everyone could complete the collage. The results are put up on the wall and Mrs. Meier gives some introducing words on the coming presentation round 5–7 min. are assigned to each.

The following time is dedicated primarily to the presentations of each participant, respectively concluded by group feed back or answering questions. Second, the quality and ways of presenting are made a topic, by connecting to examples of entrepreneurs as role models. Mrs. Meier visualizes some of the commonly collected attributes for 'good presentations' on the board. She finally widens the discussion and encourages also reflecting on the earlier activity of making the collages, on feelings, on cooperation modes, on the conflict which arose and how it was settled. In-group work conclusions for own entrepreneurial activities and activities for the training (e.g. time planning) are drawn.

'Mini Market Exercise'

We are returning to the class room Wednesday morning, to observe the role play called 'Mini Market'. Tables are arranged in a U-shape. Martin, the trainer here, has prepared an instruction chart, and behind him a lot of material: sheets of paper, magazines, scissors, pearls, buttons and other small items. He opens the session and introduces the exercise as an opportunity to develop basic marketing skills and customer-orientation. He points to the instruction chart and explains the rules:

- Sell an item to the buyer
- You have three possibilities:
    1. To sell an item owned by you
    2. To sell an item you produce
    3. To sell a service (no promises) which can be realised within 3 min
- You have 15 min. for deciding what to sell, eventually produce it and for preparing your sales presentation
- Only three products or services will be bought paying cash
- Maximum price is 3 EUR
- It will be a real buying-selling transaction
- Sold items are not returned or exchanged afterwards
- You must not sell at a loss
- You have 2 min. for your sales presentation

Martin continues with clarifying his role acting as a buyer. He will buy no more than three items at the end of the game, and he will pay cash. He won't waste much time to listening to odd sales presentations, and never more than 2 min. And, when he buys, this will be a real purchase. As observers, we leave the room at this stage. Later on we learn from a participant that the exercise had been used also to develop an instrument called 'SWOT' out from the experience from the role play.

'Working with the SWOT Grid'

It is Monday after the lunch break, in the second week of the course. Basic work experiences with the SWOT analysis had already been made in the first week, out from a role play and by applying it on a 'personal SWOT'. Today the participants are assigned to work out a SWOT for their business idea.

After opening the SWOT-method is repeated by the participants, supported by the facilitator Thomas Jopp, a strategy consultant for SME. The group work leads to the identification of the basic SWOT grid, and most participants still remember what kind of information is requested. One participant emphasizes that practical conclusions should be drawn. But all in all, the trainer remains doubtful if the group really seizes the SWOT as a tool to develop own practices, own actions as business people, or if some participants misinterpret it as mere analytical and theoretical exercise. Therefore, he encourages a discussion on the instrument and on the earlier experiences from the personal SWOT analysis a week ago. Have participants really been able and felt motivated to draw practical conclusions for their own life? Who did and who did not? Why? What were the hindrances? To whom did they address the earlier analysis, to themselves or to the trainer? Out from this discussion a general reflection on the SWOT tool and its practical relevance takes off, with drawing common conclusions on how to make better use of the SWOT. This is completed by a board visualization of basic steps for effective work with the SWOT concept (Fig. 4).

The session continues with the assignment to work out SWOT grids and real-life personal conclusions for the individual business ideas. The group chooses one business idea onto which they want to apply the SWOT within group work first, before going into the individual work. (And again, we leave as observers the room.)

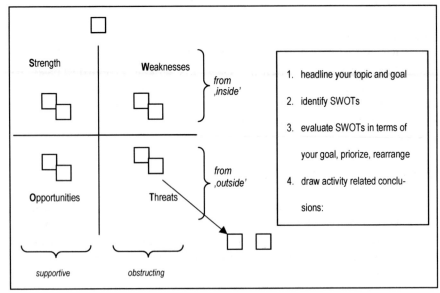

Fig. 4 Working with the SWOT grid – board visualization

References

Braun G, Diensberg C, Mechthold-Jin M (1998) Mut zur Selbständigkeit, Gründungstraining und Gründungsforschung am Institut für Human Resource Development (Courage for Self-Employment. Entrepreneurship Training and Research at the Institute for HRD), in: Traditio et Innovatio, Forschungsmagazin der Universität Rostock, 3, 1, pp. 13–16

Braun G, Diensberg C (2001) Grundlagen der Gründerqualifizierung. Planung und Einbettung, Durchführung, Evaluation (Basics of Entrepreneurship Education: Planning, Embedding, Evaluating), FernUniversität Gesamthochschule in Hagen

CEFE (2007) http://www.cefe.net/products/case/214622.htm (25 December 2007)

Göbel S, Frese M (1999) Persönlichkeit, Strategien und Erfolg bei Kleinunternehmern (Personality, strategies and success in small scale entrepreneurs), in: Moser K., Batinic B., Zempel J. (eds.): Unternehmerisch erfolgreiches Handeln, Göttingen: Hogrefe, pp. 93–113

GTZ (2000) Gesellschaft für Technische Zusammenarbeit, CEFE – International: Trainer Manual, Eschborn

Kolb DA (1984) Experiential learning: Experience as the source of learning and development. Englewood Cliffs: Prentice Hall

Revans R (1980) Action learning: New techniques for management. London: Blond & Briggs

Wilde K (2005) Kompetenz für Komplexität? – Ergebnisse der Studentenbefragung in Rostock 2003. Eine Studie von ROXI, Rostocker Existenzgründer Initiative in Zusammenarbeit mit GründerFlair, Netzwerk für Existenzgründungen aus Hochschulen in Mecklenburg-Vorpommern. In: Rostocker Arbeitspapiere zu Wirtschaftsentwicklung und Human Resource Development No. 24, Universität Rostock, http://www.cefe.net

Entrepreneurship Incubators at HAMK University of Applied Sciences

H. Hannula[*] and S. Pajari-Stylman

HAMK University of Applied Sciences, Hämeenlinna, Finland

Introduction

The Hämeenlinna sub region in Finland provides a stimulating environment for students and enterprises. Schools, universities, enterprises and Häme Development Centre Ltd. have built a network to promote entrepreneurial activities in the Hämeenlinna sub region. Entrepreneurship education is offered in state schools and vocational institutions. The objective is to promote and achieve entrepreneurship readiness at every level. Comprehensive and upper secondary schools foster entrepreneurship-friendly values and attitudes meaning to promote familiarity with entrepreneurship as a concept. Vocational institutes raise awareness for entrepreneurship as a career, teaching the basics of business operation. HAMK University of Applied Sciences and University of Tampere promote knowledge of and encourage entrepreneurship activities. Opportunities of the Hämeenlinna sub region are development of entrepreneurship education and also co-operation between regional business service organizations and regional vocational institutions and universities (Häme Development Centre Ltd.).

HAMK University of Applied Sciences offers high-quality education, research and development services, and an international atmosphere. Situated centrally in the prime area of southern Finland, HAMK has units in seven locations with 25 degree programmes and 7,000 students. The main aim is to develop a range of competences that can be utilized by businesses, industry and the public sector in the region as well as globally. HAMK's centres of expertise, developed in cooperation with companies and municipalities, support our degree programmes as well as research and

P.C. van der Sijde et al. (eds.), *Teaching Entrepreneurship.*
© Physica-Verlag Berlin Heidelberg 2008

further education. Most degree programmes at HAMK are delivered in Finnish, and some are delivered in English, among these the International Business programme.

HAMK University of Applied Sciences launched pre-incubator activities in seven of its units from 1 January 2004. The HAMK Pre-incubator activities have been developed systematically and in close co-operation between all those involved in its activities (pre-incubator leaders, degree programme support staff and teachers). In addition to student counselling and guidance, activities include training for mentors. Five training events were organized in 2004, dealing with topics such as the status of the student, the role of the leader, student counselling at the pre-incubator, constructive assessment and finances. Training events in 2005 focused on entrepreneurship education and developed a pre-incubator strategy, networking and business co-operation. Each HAMK unit organized an open day to present and market pre-incubator activities to students, teachers, other staff members and partner enterprises (Tenhunen 2006). The objectives of pre-incubator activities are to learn about entrepreneurship by actually being involved in business. The activities are divided in three stages:

1. Learning to understand entrepreneurship
2. Learning by actually being involved in business
3. Learning to do business

The HAMK strategy of entrepreneurship is based on entrepreneurial competences, business competences and knowledge of opportunities in the environment. Entrepreneurial competences include for example entrepreneurial behaviour and entrepreneurial skills. Business competences focus on seeking the opportunities in one's professional training. Also the environment offers many possibilities that could be used for the benefit of entrepreneurship. The entrepreneurial studies should be integrated in the professional studies. Entrepreneurship needs business but is more than business. In entrepreneurial studies, the process of learning is essential. The learner is in the core. In entrepreneurial learning the point is not the content but how the learner acts. The learner is responsible for his/her learning process. Different kinds of projects, on the job learning, learning by doing, action learning and incubating, offer the learning environment that enables learning the entrepreneurial way. Knowing the opportunities of one's profession facilitates finding new solutions that could be the innovations and business ideas of the future.

Learning Entrepreneurial Competences

Before we describe our incubator model, we define some key concepts. It is important to understand how we believe people can learn. The first important concept is learning. We also have to consider entrepreneurship; how do we understand the dimensions of entrepreneurship? Finally, we have to understand the concept of competence. Thus, there are three basic concepts to define.

Learning

Learning, not teaching, is the basic process in entrepreneurial studies at HAMK University of Applied Sciences. We apply a constructivist view on learning. The main task of a teacher is to support the learning of his/her students or other learners. Instead of distributors of information, knowledge or skills, the teachers are more tutors, mentors or counsellors who try to ensure that the students get good and motivating learning experiences and that they reflect on these in interactions and in collaboration with their tutors and peers. In vocational and professional learning the learning experiences should be as authentic as possible. That is why we believe in the constructive ways of learning modelled by for example in Learning by Doing, Project Learning, Action Learning, Problem-Based Learning, and Entrepreneurial Learning etc. We believe in applying several learning models, but in this article we just use action learning as an example. There are not one or two ways of learning. Every learner is a unique person who learns in a personal way. That is why we think learning and teaching should be as personalized as possible. The basis of a learning process is the mental models of a learner. We try to help and support our learners to find out the best ways of changing and developing their mental models to enable vocational and professional growth. How to support the learning process? Effective methods of supporting learning should employ various didactical and pedagogical forms. There are several ways of learning both formally, informally and non-formally. Studying, doing, observing, group working etc. are examples how to experience learning. The learners should know why to work and what to do to reach the set objectives. For example, at the end of the studies or after the studies, the incubation of the ideas is a very efficient learning method. However, before reaching that stage many other methods should have been used.

Entrepreneurship

Entrepreneurship is a wide concept. It means not only entrepreneurship as an entrepreneur. It means individual entrepreneurship, organizational entrepreneurship and intrapreneurship, as well. Kyrö and Carrier (2005) define these four issues in the following way:

1. The oldest form of individual, self-oriented entrepreneurship, meaning an individual's self-oriented behaviour (entrepreneurial behaviour).
2. The creation, management and ownership of a small enterprise, referring to the individual entrepreneur and his enterprise (entrepreneurship).
3. Corporate or organizational entrepreneurship referring to an organization's collective behaviour (organizational entrepreneurship), and finally.
4. Intrapreneurship referring to the interplay between individual and organizational entrepreneurship.

Entrepreneurship is both creating and doing business and a way of working. Business creation aims at fulfilling the needs of customers. It means that "the entrepreneur" has to connect to and co-operate with different kinds of people. We can call this entrepreneurial behaviour. But entrepreneurship can also appear when one is an employee or pursuing a hobby. Gibb (2005) also calls this entrepreneurial behaviour. He means by entrepreneurial behaviours:

- Opportunity seeking and grasping
- Taking initiatives to make things happen
- Solving problems creatively
- Managing autonomously
- Taking responsibility for, and ownership of, things
- Seeing things through
- Networking effectively to manage interdependence
- Putting things together creatively
- Using judgement to take calculated risks

Thus, authors vary in their definitions of entrepreneurship. For example, according to Koiranen and Ruohotie (2001) entrepreneurship is a holistic, responsible and innovative way of thinking, acting and being in one's professional life. It can be seen as a person's affective, conative, and cognitive mental properties. In the cognitive area there are for example skills and the knowledge. But we can see values and attitudes in entrepreneurship in the affective area as well and we can distinguish motivational aspects and orientations in the conative area. (Snow et al. 1994) All of these things determine entrepreneurship and should therefore be paid attention to. On the other hand entrepreneurship is strongly associated with the abilities to recognize the opportunities in the environment and to exploit them (Kyrö and Carrier 2005; Carrier 2005; Gibb 2005). That means especially the ability to see and sketch different states of affairs in the future. A man should also believe in his own influence on the things that will happen. In other words we need self-efficacy (Heinonen and Paasio 2005). The concept of opportunity includes the possibility that things go in a planned way. But it also includes the threat that things will not. This implies that the concept of risk is also strongly associated with entrepreneurship. Entrepreneurs should be able to live with uncertainty (Kyrö 2006). To conclude we present the definition that describes our thinking: *Entrepreneurship is not only being or becoming an entrepreneur. It is holistic, visionary, innovative, responsible and proactive action with other people to recognize and exploit opportunities; and entrepreneurship can be learnt in an entrepreneurial way.*

Competence

Competence means not only the knowledge, skills and mental qualities of a human being that drives him/her in work. Helakorpi (2007) lists, that:

- Competence is both individual and social.
- Competence is a result of both formal, informal and non-formal learning.
- Competence in not only knowledge or skills but it is seen more and more as managing the actions including especially the social interaction.
- Competence includes flexibility, living with insecurity and willingness to change and to be changed.
- Competence is continuous assessment and development.
- Competence is linked to the context and the culture.

The objectives of learning should be the competences. We could define these as "The student is able to discover the possibilities in his/her vocation." It means for example that during their studies the students learn to explore different possibilities to get employed. They may make real products and try to sell them to real customers. They are allowed to take calculated risks and have some insecurity in their studies, and so on. A very important point is also that assessments should be targeted to meet the set objectives, the competences. As mentioned, a method or learning environment to learn entrepreneurial competences is to support the ideas of the students in an entrepreneurship incubator. At HAMK University of Applied Sciences there are several incubators and in the following paragraphs we will present them as case-based teaching, or "case-based learning in entrepreneurship education."

Entrepreneurship Learning at HAMK University of Applied Sciences Pre-incubator

A pre-incubator is a learning environment providing students with opportunities to complete entrepreneurship studies, projects and work placement and prepare their own Bachelor's thesis relating to product development, business plans, marketing or developing their own business operations. Pre-incubators provide learning through reflection and experience. Learning is problem-based, self-directed, goal-oriented and action-based learning by doing. Pre-incubator activities aim to increase awareness of entrepreneurship and business activities.

The HAMK pre-incubators and Action Learning as a pedagogical process (see Fig. 1) help students choose study units aiming at setting up and

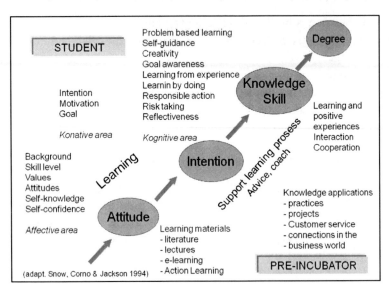

Fig. 1 Learning process at HAMK pre-incubator

running a business. Pre-incubator activities support students' learning process through counselling, guiding and training them towards the world of entrepreneurship by interactive and community-based means.

The objective of the incubation activities at HAMK is to learn about entrepreneurship and to learn by actually being involved in business. The activities are divided in three stages (Saurio 2003), see Fig. 2 below:

Fig. 2 Learning process in entrepreneurship

The specification clarifies the objectives of HAMK incubation activities. The municipal business incubators are left with the tasks of further developing and supporting business start-ups, i.e. learning to do business after graduation. Thus the primary indicator for the pre-incubator activities' successes is not the number of enterprises created, but the quality of the activities and the number of students and studies completed within a pre-incubator's learning environment. A pre-incubator is, first and foremost, a learning environment for studying entrepreneurship and business activities. Targets at the pre-incubator at HAMK are to further develop older and support the creation of new product- and business ideas. The aim is that students after graduation start up profitable and competitive businesses.

Using real life cases students learn about entrepreneurship, for entrepreneurship and even through entrepreneurship. Students learn about entrepreneurship and intrapreneurship, by visiting entrepreneurs or by training in enterprises. When learning for entrepreneurship, students work on projects and business cases with enterprises. Students learn how to create new business models, and how to price and market products and services. They learn how to build partnerships and networks during their studies and at the same time develop their social and interactional skills. Most students at the pre-incubator have clients and business cases in regional companies. Students for example produce websites for companies or make and sell products they have designed and manufactured. At its best, students combine their vocational education and training with entrepreneurship education and business know-how. One good example of that are two students who produce tiled fireplaces. In their vocational studies they developed ceramic tiles and at the pre-incubator they learnt how to price and market the fireplaces they designed and make a business plan. After graduation they indeed started up a company with their own designed and manufactured fireplaces.

The Action Learning method has formed a key part of pre-incubator pedagogy in HAMK University of applied sciences. Action Learning method is a student-centred way of learning. Applied here, it is about development of business ideas and of the students themselves. Development is accomplished in a form applied to each student's own needs, in a practical manner and by solving real-life problems. By working in a small multidisciplinary 'set' (group), students receive constructive feedback for their actions, new insights and encouraging support from their peer group. The multidisciplinary nature of sets has been considered to be useful, because it allows students to receive feedback both from students specializing in other fields and from those studying the same field. At the same time, Action Learning set participants' self-knowledge and perception of other people's behaviour increase, while their ability to ask questions, listen and converse improves. Action Learning has made it possible to achieve successful learning experiences. Action Learning sets have produced clear and immediate benefits for development of students' own enterprises or business plans. Students have learnt to ask questions and listen to other people as well as to provide and receive constructive feedback. They have time to think and reflect on their own views between set meetings. Many have adopted a new, questioning approach to their work. In addition, pre-incubator students have also put together personal study plans to support and develop their own pathways towards entrepreneurship. The most important work of a teacher is to manage the whole process. It means both the learning processes of the student and the processes that give support for the learning processes. They have to create the learning environments the way they can offer the real learning experiences to the students. But the teachers have to manage also the reflection of the experiences. The main objective for the students is to develop as an entrepreneur. And the teachers have to give to the students all the support that need go towards to the goal.

Examples of tools:

Pre-incubators may perform a *Thomas Personal Profile Analysis* for students in the final stages of their studies, which provides them with personal feedback both orally and in writing. The Thomas analysis aims to give an objective and structured overview of a student's communication and behavioural style at work. Feedback allows students to improve their self-knowledge and self-esteem. At the same time, students have also received constructive feedback about functioning as an entrepreneur, their communication styles and their supervisory and sales skills. To date, the HAMK pre-incubators have done Thomas analyses for about twenty students.

The *HAMK Starttihautomo co-operative* was established in the spring of 2004. The co-operative is a company supporting pre-incubator studies and students' entrepreneurial activities, where students can safely practise business operations while studying, without losing their student status or benefits. The purpose of the co-operative is to function as a marketing channel for pre-incubator students' own business ideas, their own products or the products and services of a potential business enterprise and as a platform for practical entrepreneurship training.

The *Sense business plan competition* aims to kick off new business ideas, teach about business planning, innovations, human capital and networks and produce additional positive energy for work, growth, learning and life in general (www.sense.hamk.fi). The idea behind the Sense competition is to provide expert lectures at the beginning of the competition followed by a brainstorming and writing process to support students and finally public presentation of the entries. Sense is an open business plan competition, which has been organized ever since 2001. Participation in various business plan competitions supports students in their entrepreneurship studies.

Action Learning

The Action Learning method, compared with traditional learning, means learning what you need at the right time versus learning what you might need some time. Learning is to do something in a new way. Learning is based on changes. Learning is happening by changing your way of thinking, modifying your way to act, to behave and to co-operate. The three main questions in the action learning process are:

1. Who knows something about the problem?
2. Who cares if the problem is solved, in other words to whom are the change important?
3. Who can do something to the problem? (Grönfors 2002)

The father of Action Learning method, Revans (1998), said that "There is no learning without action and no sober and deliberate action without learning." He thinks that individuals' active participation is the key to learning. Analysis of your own and other people's actions and reflection on and assessment of the real situation lead to learning. Learning from different views and ways of thinking and learning by doing means that people are learning to learn. The learning process is lifelong and people are learning from real-life problems (Grönfors 2002). Action Learning is a process where individuals learn together and from each other by sharing experiences. Individuals learn to recognize, analyze and process real problems and opportunities through participation. They reflect on their own and other people's thoughts, feelings and actions. Participants help, support and question other people's mental models and encourage new ways of thinking, viewpoints and implementing each participant's own alternative solutions. Individuals exchange ideas and test solutions by focusing more on questions than on offering solutions. Advice is only given on request. Participants are helped to solve their problems themselves rather than solving them on their behalf. The set's drawbacks are addressed frankly, people learn teamwork and networking. Groups and organizations are helped to gain a deeper understanding that allows them to work efficiently now and in the future. Participants take responsibility for their own learning. The identified learning and development methods can easily be transferred to new processes (Grönfors 2002). The set advisor's (teacher) expertise is available but not forced. It is provided in suitable 'doses' at the right time and in the right conditions.

Sets are groups of 5–7 people, who meet regularly in set meetings, to learn with and from each other (composition should preferably not change during the programme). Participation in the set must be voluntary. Members work on their own topics, tasks or projects. Set learning takes time; unlearning old things, repetition, reflection on action, real-life projects. Trust and openness need time to develop. Conflicts can occur in set meetings (different personalities, feelings, expectations, behavioural styles – tolerance of diversity, new potential solutions, patience and a positive approach). But by asking and changing ways of thinking and acting these will be solved. The set advisor is a learning facilitator, moderator, tutor, counsellor, mentor, team leader or assessor of set members' work. He/she helps the set to help themselves and make progress as they learn. The facilitator does not solve problems or make decisions for set members but helps question beliefs, perceptions and presumptions. Set advisors encourage members to listen, ask, understand and learn. He/she draws attention to learning opportunities: 'What have you learnt?' and focuses on the team-work process; reflects on the process, encourages, supports, stimulates and provides feedback elegantly (Grönfors 2002). The Action Learning process is represented in Fig. 3.

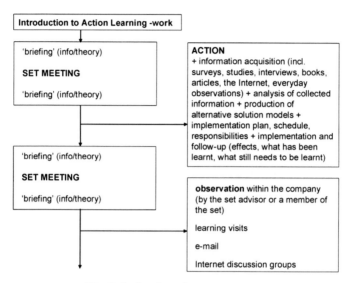

Fig. 3 Action learning process

Conclusions

In this chapter we presented our ideas and activities concerning learning entrepreneurship. In 2004, 85 students were doing their studies at the HAMK pre-incubator. After three years, the amount of students has grown to 202. In 2007, students set up eight new enterprises after graduation and they have employed ten people. The new companies are in the fields of design and handicraft, information technology and services. Students in HAMK agriculture and horticulture programmes mainly continue their family business or sometimes set up business of their own. Entrepreneurial intentions progress during life-long-learning. Learning entrepreneurial competences is based on personal competences and social processes. It means that learners should reflect on their own experiences, but mostly in social context with other learners. Pre-incubators offer excellent contexts for this. The most important work of a teacher is to manage the whole process. It means both the learning processes of the student and the pro-cesses that give support for the learning processes. Teachers have to create the optimal learning environments, give the students all the support that is needed to go towards to the goal, and manage the students' reflections on the experiences. Pre-incubator activities help students to change their intentions to real activities in entrepreneurship.

References

Carrier C (2005) Pedagogical challenges in entrepreneurship education. In Kyrö, P. and Carrier C (Eds.) The Dynamics of Learning Entrepreneurship in a Cross-Cultural University Context. Entrepreneurship Education Series 2/2005. University of Tampere. Faculty of Education. Research Center for Vocational and Professional Education

Gibb A (2005) The future of entrepreneurship education – Determining the basis for coherent policy and practice? In Kyrö, P. and Carrier, C. (Eds.) The Dynamics of Learning Entrepreneurship in a Cross-Cultural University Context. Entrepreneurship Education Series 2/2005. University of Tampere. Faculty of Education. Research Center for Vocational and Professional Education

Grönfors T (2002) Työstä oppiminen – Action Learning, Työssä oppiminen – e-learning. Vantaa 2002. Facile Publishing

Häme Developing Centre Ltd. Retrieved October 30, 2007, from http://www.kehittamiskeskus.com

HAMK University of Applied Sciences. Retrieved May 24, 2007, from http://portal.hamk.fi/portal/page/portal/HAMK/In_English/About_HAMK

Heinonen J, Paasio K (2005) Sisäinen yrittäjyys kuntatyössä. Kunnallisalan kehittämissäätiön tutkimusjulkaisut nro 48

Helakorpi S. Osaaminen ja sen arviointi. Retrieved May 23, 2007, from http://openetti.aokk.fi/seppoh/osaamismittarit/index.htm

Koiranen M, Ruohotie P (2001) Yrittäjyyskasvatus: analyyseja, synteesejä ja sovelluksia. Aikuiskasvatus 2/2001

Kyrö P (2006) New Generation Business Planning INTERNATIONAL BEPART SYMPOSIUM Innovative Actions in Entrepreneurship Education & Training 8–9 June 2006 University of Rostock, Germany Track A: Business Plan Oriented Teaching & Use of E-Learning. New Generation Business Planning

Kyrö P, Carrier C (2005) Entrepreneurial learning in universities: Bridges across borders. In Kyrö, P. and Carrier, C. (Eds.) The Dynamics of Learning Entrepreneurship in a Cross-Cultural University Context. Entreprenreurship Education Series 2/2005. University of Tampere. Faculty of Education. Research Center for Vocational and Professional Education

Revans R (1998) ABC of Action Learning – Empowering Managers to Act and to Learn from Action. London, UK, Lemos and Crane

Saurio S (2003) Yrittäjyyden edistäminen ja yrityshautomotoiminta ammattikorkeakouluympäristössä. Satakunnan ammattikorkeakoulu, A, tutkimukset 1/ 2003. Pori: Satakunnan ammattikorkeakoulu

Snow R.E, Corno L, Jackson D (1994) Individual differences in affective and conative functions. In Berliner, D.C. and Calfee, R.C. (Eds.), Handbook of Educational Psychology. New York. Simon and Schuster Macmillan, pp. 243–310

Tenhunen L (2006) Starttihautomokonsepti Hämeen ammattikorkeakoulussa. Teoksessa Kyrö, P. and Ripatti, A. (Eds.) Yrittäjyyskasvatuksen uusia tuulia. Yrittäjyyskasvatuksen julkaisusarja 4/2006, Tampereen yliopiston kauppakorkeakoulu, Hämeenlinna 132–145

The Entrepreneurship Path Model: Promoting Entrepreneurship in Kainuu

P. Malinen[*] and P. Partanen

Kajaani University of Applied Sciences, Kajaani, Finland

Introduction

The development of entrepreneurial attitudes and entrepreneurial skills is high on the list of regional targets. In the future Kainuu will need more and more entrepreneurial personalities who are creative, independent and self-confident solution seekers possessing good taste, good social skills and a capacity for independent thinking. According to research, 49% of students studying at Kajaani University of Applied Sciences (UAS) are interested in entrepreneurial activities. To promote students' entrepreneurship skills Kajaani UAS cooperates with pre-incubator Intotalo (http://www.intotalo.com). Intotalo is a special training organisation which prepares local young people for starting businesses of their own. The development of entrepreneurship within the local authority of Kajaani is the responsibility of the Kajaani Technology Centre Oy/Business Development Department. The Business Incubator (Entrepreneurship Training Centre) Intotalo is responsible for supporting and organising training for recently established and new businesses. Intotalo has been operating in Kajaani since the beginning of 2003. During the autumn of 2005 Intotalo also started operating in Vuokatti within the vicinity of Snowpolis.

It has been necessary to find new ways of working and to carry out widespread cooperation between different parties in order to meet the challenges posed by entrepreneurship in the region. The aim of such cooperation has been to create structures and support networks to make starting up a business easier for new entrepreneurs. The goal is to enthuse university graduates to start out in business. Intotalo started as an ESF funded project and its operations became permanent in 2006. Thus a permanent and

P.C. van der Sijde et al. (eds.), *Teaching Entrepreneurship*.
© Physica-Verlag Berlin Heidelberg 2008

successful cooperation model and structure have been created in Kainuu that involves Intotalo, Kajaani University of Applied Sciences and other educational institutions and businesses.

Learning Environment-Business Incubator Intotalo (Intohouse)

Kajaani UAS entrepreneurship path's main learning environment is the Intotalo Business Incubator. Intotalo is a learning environment that advances learning in skills required in project work and running a business. Learning in the Intotalo is based on constructivism i.e. learning by doing. The learning process can also be described as a combining of theoretical and practical knowledge and self-knowledge. According to research, project work and learning by doing effectively promote the development of an individual's business skills and above all, generate an entrepreneurial attitude. The most important value of the Intotalo is its community. It strives to create an atmosphere and environment where small businesses can work together instead of alone. Through such a community it is easy for businesses to network with other companies and active parties in the Kainuu region. Start-up entrepreneurs and entrepreneurship students have had positive experiences of the Intotalo at the outset of their business activities. They received valuable help from others in creating their own customers and other practical issues related to running their own businesses.

Intotalo is Kajaani UAS' business incubator. The aim is to recognise and find potential entrepreneurial personalities from the different fields of Kajaani UAS and offer them the opportunity to develop their own business ideas in practice. The target is to ensure that cooperation between Kajaani UAS and Intotalo will lead to 5% of all graduates from Kajaani UAS establishing their own companies within 5 years of graduation. Students are able to test their own ideas and skills in practice via their studies and the business incubator organised by Kajaani UAS and Kajaani Intotalo. It is intended that ten start-up businesses will be found for the business incubator per year. The entrepreneurship path is in Kajaani UAS's curricula (see Fig. 1, next page). Basic entrepreneurship information is provided in all faculties as compulsory studies. For example all students make a "short business plan" at the beginning of their studies, but the main idea of this business plan is that the students can combine materials and thoughts from different kinds of courses into a more integrated idea of what the business is about. The actual entrepreneurship studies are then implemented through students' personal choices.

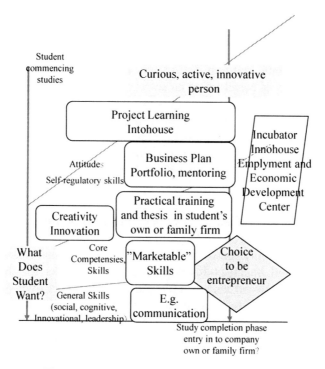

Fig. 1 Entrepreneurship path in Kajaani UAS

Students can choose project studies in all faculties in order to gain more in-depth professional skills in developing raw business ideas. The pedagogic model relies on the developmental transfer approach and on combining theoretical, practical and self-regulation knowledge into expertise. In the most outstanding projects, students carry out the entire product development cycle that ranges from customer needs to a tested product. This is the same process that entrepreneurs complete when planning and developing their business.

The student can draw up a portfolio-type of business plan targeted at setting up an own company. This will help him/her start the business after the completion of studies and entitle him/her to assistance from other support organisations, for instance the Employment and Economic Development Centre. All business plans are tailored according to students' needs and teaching is arranged using the mentoring method. The teaching method used is Problem Based Learning (PBL). The course can also be done in Intotalo environment or only based on the tutorship of the student and tutoring teacher. Of course there are always mentors involved in the process. During this course PBL ends up pointing students toward sense-making over fact-collecting, as it always should do. It is learning as a result from working with (some) problems. What students learn about collaboration, different approaches to a problem, cooperation and responsibility, makes their learning during this PBL course all-round, rich and deep. The process of constructing an entrepreneurial business plan addresses the following goals: presentation skills (written and oral), effective thinking and reasoning, research skills, analytic problem solving using the knowledge of business functions, synthetic thinking-seeing relationships between business functions in a firm, formulating creative options and deciding appropriate strategies, clarity on personal strengths and career goals, and, holistic development.

The UAS studies include 5 months of practical training, depending on the field of education. The student can also complete the training in his/her own company or family company. The student, company and tutoring teacher draw up personal business-development learning tasks for the training period. The student can also complete the thesis in his own or a family company. The tutoring teacher and the student together decide on the company's aspects of business to be developed. Every spring Intotalo organises an open business idea competition in which participating Kajaani UAS students can develop their business ideas with the help of Intotalo's network of mentors. This support will be focussed on the best business ideas presented to the selection panel. The main competition entrance requirement is that the idea can be implemented in Northern Finland.

Overview of Courses

Project Studies/Practical Training in a Student or Family Owned Company

- *Process*: Learning by projects. Students make project plans and decide which processes will be developed during the project or practical training.
- *Media/means*: Tutorials, students' active role, mentors from firms and entrepreneurship promotion organisations.
- *Goals*: Students will have more mature business plans when graduating and can get access to the Incubator Intohouse for example, or they know what further education or work experience they need before the start-up.
- *Entrepreneurial phase*: Start-up stage or in family business the change of the generation.

- *Target group*: Students in their third or fourth study year, at the end of their studies. Students who have taken the project courses have been in the faculty of social sciences, business and administration.

Portfolio Type Business Plan

- *Process*: Lasts about 1 year, stages correspond to the PBL method (see Fig. 2). At the beginning of the semester there are group tutorials but mainly tutor teachers and students discuss privately
- *Media/means*: Tutorials, students' active role, mentors from firms and entrepreneurship promotion organisations

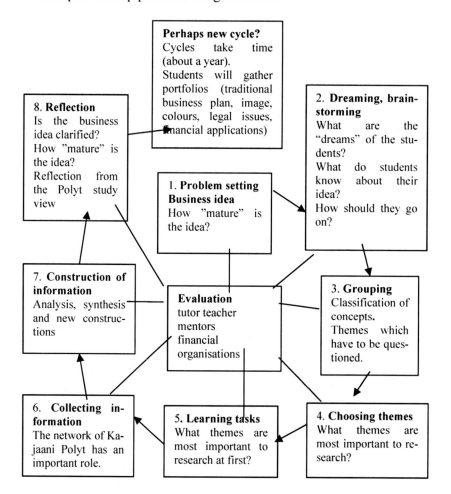

Fig. 2 Modified cycles of PBL in the context of the business plan course

- *Goals*: Students will have mature business plans when graduating or they know what further education or work experience they might need before start-up
- *Entrepreneurial phase*: Feasibility stage. Making the business idea more accurate, not yet really start-up stage. The portfolio helps them to deal with Incubators outside UAS and to get finance
- *Target group*: Students in their third or fourth study year, at the end of their studies, all faculties

Business Incubator Courses: The Entrepreneurship Path

Study modules	Contents description
Innoste-business idea competition	A regional business idea competition open to all UAS students for the purpose of seeking business, product and service concepts for further development. The ideas and concepts under development presented during this competition can also be entered in the national Venture Cup business concept competition.
Entrepreneurship course	Students will gain a realistic view of their own opportunities and make contacts with other businesses in the region through different commissions and jobs. Students will determine common aims for their own entrepreneurial skill development in teams. It comprises team training sessions, reading and practical business ventures.
Business plan	Students must compile their own business plan based on their business idea in collaboration with the Intotalo trainer and UAS instructor/teacher. Each student will contact a mentor for support and encouragement in the development of their own businesses.
Practical training in entrepreneurship	During the practical training period students develop their own businesses according to their business plan. They will try out whether they can successfully operate a profitable business venture. The practical training period consists of practical customer – commissioned projects, compiling a business foundation plan and development work in cooperation with the Intotalo trainers and an experienced mentor. Intotalo provides the students with workstations and supportive encouragement to develop their theses.
Entrepreneurship thesis	The students must complete a thesis that includes a practical analysis of the business they have/are to create and their market areas using applied theory. Intotalo provides a workstation as well as encouragement and support.

Business Incubator Courses: The Postgraduate Path

Modules	Contents description
Incubator training	The target group of the business incubator includes graduates planning to go into business and small businesses that have recently started operating and that have a "brilliant idea" or wish to make the most of the opportunities that are on offer in the locality. The training course comprises entrepreneurship training sessions, the practical realisation of their business ventures and mentoring. The training course lasts 1–6 months.
Entrepreneurship sparring partners and mentors	Intotalo's trainers spar on those planning their own business ventures to develop their own knowledge, networks and customer contacts. UAS students can also take advantage of the Intotalo mentor network. Those who are planning their own businesses can also try out their first customer contacts through the Intotalo Cooperative.
Entrepreneur community	Intotalo offers new entrepreneurs workstations, office infrastructure to support the development of their business and communal support. The business trainers provide support in compiling the business plan and marketing. The managing directors of the Intotalo companies meet once a month at their own development and strategy evening.

Results of Cooperation 2003–2006

As a result of the common entrepreneurship path, eight new businesses have been established over the last 3 years by UAS graduates. The aim is to further develop such operations and discover five new budding businesses each year. These activities, that originally started as part of a project became permanent on January 1, 2006.

Master Program in Entrepreneurship and Technology Management in Estonia

J. Andrijevskaja[*] and T. Mets

Centre for Entrepreneurship, Faculty of Economics and Business Administration, University of Tartu, Tartu, Estonia

Introduction

A wide range of universities and colleges have recently invested in developing programs in entrepreneurship and technology management. Striving for entrepreneurial knowledge economies and supported politically, many institutions have successfully introduced a curriculum either in technology management or entrepreneurship. However, the examples of successful curricula, where entrepreneurship and technology management are integrated, are not so numerous. According to a 2001 European Commission's report, there are major problems related to entrepreneurial education:

1. Entrepreneurship programs are not supported on political level, and are weakly integrated into educational system.
2. The evaluation system of entrepreneurship education is inadequate.
3. At universities, entrepreneurship is mostly taught to business students.
4. Teachers are not sufficiently trained to become entrepreneur.
5. Weak relations among universities and business sector diminish effectiveness of teaching entrepreneurship.

The list of problems indicates that the difficulties can be in the launching stage (due to lack of experience, lack of political and financial support), but also when insuring a good quality of courses and their correspondence to the needs of entrepreneurs. Indeed, even the United Kingdom, a country known for its pro-business environment, high-quality MBA and entrepreneurship programs, is criticized for inefficient entrepreneurship teaching methods. Numerous UK entrepreneurship programs lack structure and

P.C. van der Sijde et al. (eds.), *Teaching Entrepreneurship.*
© Physica-Verlag Berlin Heidelberg 2008

clear objectives, institutions prefer investing in advertising innovative programs rather than raising the quality of a curriculum. In many institutions the established academic traditions are a serious obstacle for entrepreneurial programs to be launched, thus new initiatives face tremendous resistance. (Tiratsoo 2004). Problems of entrepreneurship and technology management education are discussed by Weller and Dhillon (1999), who mentions that lecturers often choose a specialist approach, not integrating a particular course with other courses, or not integrating theory with business or another type of environment.

The University of Tartu (Estonia) has been the first university in the Baltic States to deal with the above and integrate entrepreneurship and technology management in a master program curriculum. The objective of the program is to provide modern and applicable knowledge in entrepreneurship, innovation and technology management, so that in the long run the master program will help Estonian companies to become more innovative and technology oriented. Having started in 2002, the program still has some challenges to overcome, but it is clear that the initiative has a strong demand in Estonia. The objective of this chapter is not only to describe the program, but also evaluate the extent to which the master program succeeds in providing modern and applicable knowledge in entrepreneurship, innovation and technology for the managers of small high-tech companies. The reason for focusing on small high-tech companies is that managers of these companies are considered one of the main target groups for the master program. The next section gives an overview of the Entrepreneurship and Technology Management (ETM) program, followed by an assessment of the needs of high-tech companies, and finishes with results and conclusions (see Fig. 1, next page).

ETM Master Program: Overview and Potential Challenges

The ETM master program at the University of Tartu was first opened for enrolment in 2002. The initial objective of the program persisted until now – it is to integrate studies in entrepreneurship and technology management and raise the "...entrepreneurial culture in the academic community" (Final Report on Development of Master Programme in Entrepreneurship and Technology Management 2001). Launching the ETM curriculum was a pioneering initiative in the Baltic States: up to today, there are no institutions either in Estonia or in other Baltic States that run similar programs.

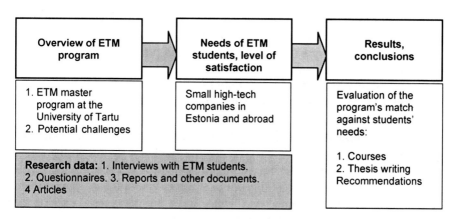

Fig. 1 Structure of this chapter

The program was developed by the international team of experts belonging to the International Association of Science Parks. The advantage of the pioneering group was a good knowledge of technology management (Tallinn University of Technology) and extensive entrepreneurial experience (Zernike Group). Both knowledge and experience were helpful in applying for PHARE funds to develop the curriculum in detail. The main structure of the ETM master program (Table 1) was developed in 2001 and remained largely unchanged until now.

Table 1 EMT master program at the University of Tartu

Criteria	Description
Nominal study time	2 years
Volume of the program	80 credit points (CP) or 120 CP according to ECTS
Entrance criteria	Bachelor degree in natural sciences, engineering, economics or social sciences
Structure of the program	56 CP for ETM obligatory and non-obligatory courses 20 CP – Master Thesis 4 CP – courses under other faculties
Modules in the program	Entrepreneurship Technology and Innovation Electives Management of Innovative SMEs Free choice of courses Master Thesis
Study time schedules	Classes once a month, over long weekends: Thursday through Sunday
Number of enrolled students	2002: 25 students; 2003: 30 students, 2004: 35 students

After introduction of the curriculum, the faculty formed a council for the development of ETM program. The council consisted of four people: two professors and two students' representatives. As planned, the ETM master program had an international and interdisciplinary character from the very first days of its establishment. Not only teachers from Estonian universities taught ETM, but also experts from Zernike Group (The Netherlands), International University of Entrepreneurship (The Netherlands), and Michigan Technological University (USA). The target group of the master program are specialists who have received a Bachelor degree in the fields of natural sciences, engineering, economics or social sciences. In the selection of applicants, the priority is given to students with the background from natural sciences and engineering. Other criteria are managerial experience and a strong motivation for entrepreneurial activities. The program's nominal study time is 2 years. In 2004 the first four students graduated. During the following year six more students obtained an ETM Master Diploma. In 2005 the program went through the accreditation process at the Estonian Ministry of Education. The ETM master program enjoys a growing number of students and a favourable public image. Nevertheless, considering the experience of other countries it might be expected that there might be serious challenges facing this pioneering curriculum.

Educational Needs of Small High-Tech Companies

After a long period of planned economy, Estonia gained independence in 1991, having faced the need for restructuring of partly collapsed industries and raising competitiveness of newly established businesses. Even though the government is trying to improve business environment in Estonia, there are yet numerous problems that hold the ratio of start-ups and innovative companies at the level below EU average. What educational needs do small high-tech companies have? Due to the fact, that this question is not sufficiently studied in Estonia, the experience of other countries is presented here. For example, a survey of Chiesa and Piccaluga (2000) showed that among the most critical issues for small high-tech companies were finding financing sources, applying the right marketing approach and commercializing the technology (Table 2, next page).

Table 2 Major problems of small high-tech companies

Problem	Average rating (1 unimportant – 5 critical importance)
Financing	3.58
Marketing, selling, commercialization	3.10
Evaluation of market's needs	2.73
Distribution, logistics	2.57
Technical problems in production and development of product	2.42
Problems with contracts	1.83
Managing human resource	1.78
Problems with business owner	1.62
IPR	1.54

Source: Chiesa and Piccaluga (2000)

For many Estonian technology-based companies, the local market is too small to operate without losses, thus it would be necessary for ETM educational programs to include courses on internationalization. Another important aspect discussed in literature on high-tech small businesses is a question of employees' motivation. The biggest value in innovative companies is often not just technologies, but people, who develop and commercialize technologies. Retaining and motivating these people can be challenging for manager, who has no managerial education. Summarizing the discussion above, a manager of a small high-tech company is likely to have an interest in the following educational fields: marketing, sales, internationalization, and human resource management. Additionally, it is also important to learn how to manage technology efficiently. These four fields with several keywords have been presented to several ETM students to discuss major educational needs perceived by them. The results of the discussion are presented in Table 3 (next page).

When asked about writing a Master Thesis at the university, ETM students expressed uniform opinions that the subject for the thesis needs to be closely connected to the practical issues, for example, case-solving approach or writing a business plan. Students did highly appreciate the consulting obtained by the supervisor and other parties, who were helping them to prepare the thesis. Thus not only the content of the curriculum is important for students, but also informal communication with lecturers, professors, as well as motivating and pragmatic requirements for writing a Master Thesis.

Table 3 Educational needs of small high-tech companies' managers

Field	Needs
Marketing and sales	Practical marketing skills for small high-tech company
	Mapping potential market
	Cooperation with client, communicational psychology
	Marketing in a narrow technological field
	Sales and organization of distribution network
Product development	Evaluation of commercial potential and viability of a
	Creation of a network (finance, marketing, technology
	Patents, IPR
	Product development, technology transfer
Internationalization	Contracts and international business acts
	Getting started in a narrow, but global technology field.
	Searching and choosing strategic partners
	Advertising, purchasing decisions etc in various countries
Teamwork management	Motivating employees to think in business terms
	Teamwork

Results and Conclusions

The objective of this chapter was to present the ETM master program, introduced at the University of Tartu, and to analyze to which extent the program corresponds to the needs of managers of small high-tech companies. The description of the ETM was given in the previous section, the conclusions about the program's match against students needs is to be discussed in the present section. Additional topics discussed below are the major strengths and weaknesses of the program, as well as the opportunities for further development.

The first version of ETM master program consisted of 26 courses, grouped in six modules: Entrepreneurial environment; Technology policy and management; Marketing and sales management; Financial planning and control; Legal Issues; Human recourses and communication. As the needs of the managers of small high-tech companies have been discussed earlier, it is now possible to clarify, to which extent the demanded education corresponded to the ETM master curriculum (Table 4, next page). Analyzing the match between students' educational needs and available ETM courses, it appears that most of the demanded fields are covered by the master program.

Table 4 Match between educational needs of students and available ETM courses

Field	Needs	Available ETM courses
Marketing and sales	Practical marketing skills for small high-tech company	Marketing
	Mapping potential market	Marketing
	Cooperation with client, communicational psychology	Sales and distribution management
	Marketing in a narrow technological	–
	Sales and organization of distribution network	Sales and distribution management
Product development	Evaluation of commercial potential and viability of a business idea	Application of technology strategy methods in business
	Creation of a network (finance, marketing, technology etc.)	–
	Patents, IPR	Intellectual property rights: licensing, protection of trademarks and products
	Product development, technology transfer	Technology transfer; Quality management; Nanotechnologies etc
Internationalization	Contracts and international business acts	Contract and business negotiations
	Getting started in a narrow, but global technology field.	–
	Searching and choosing strategic partners	–
	Advertising, purchasing decisions etc in various countries	Sales and distribution management; Marketing
Teamwork	Motivating employees to think in business terms	Leadership and personnel development
	Teamwork	–
	Organizational culture (acknowledgements etc)	Organizational culture

The interviews with students enabled collecting some additional information. Students with non-economic backgrounds appreciated the fact that they could enrol into the program that combines business, entrepreneurship and technological matters. It was also highly valued that most of the ETM teachers are professionals in their fields and some of them have also extensive practical experience. Dissatisfaction was caused by the fact that several technology-oriented subjects are poorly connected to business and entrepreneurship, being like scientific courses instead. There was also a comment that some of the teachers (mostly from Estonia) are reluctant to make courses interactive, and courses' information to be more applicable in business. This might be caused by: (a) teachers lack of appropriate training in modern teaching methods, (b) traditionally academic career of several local teachers (see also Tables).

Table 5 Conclusions of the study

Strengths	Weaknesses
Interdisciplinary: technology, business, entrepreneurship	Local teachers lack ability/motivation to connect theory with business reality
International network of top-specialists	Local teachers use few methods to make the course interactive
Uniqueness in Baltic States	Traditionally academic requirements to Master Thesis
Sustainable structure of courses	Lack of several essential courses
Suggestions	
Organize training seminars for current and potential ETM teachers	
Add several courses: on psychology, launching new product etc	
Invite practitioners (including ETM alumni) for short-term lecturing	
Rethink requirements for the ETM Master Thesis	
Strengthen international network and links to practitioners with academic background	

Partly, as a result of the analysis described above, initiated by professor Urmas Varblane, the project INNOEDU (Innovation Education Development, co-financed from EU structural funds) was launched in 2005. Altogether ten new courses were designed or existing courses reshaped, stressing the entrepreneurship and innovation focus of the program.

The ETM master program has been developed based on the needs of Estonian businesses. Demand for ETM education is a clearly increasing trend: intake of students started at 20–25 in 2002 has reached the level 40 in 2007. Even though there are some challenges the ETM program faces, the development council of ETM program works on improving the program by attracting new partners and raising requirements for ETM teachers. After the accreditation of the program in 2005 the discussions started to prepare a full English version of the program for international students.

This research has been partly financed by the target funding project SF0180037s08.

References

Chiesa V, Piccaluga A exploitation and diffusion of public research: the case of academic spin-off companies in Italy. R&D Management, 2000, Vol. 30, No. 4, pp. 329–339

Final Report on Development of Master Programme in Entrepreneurship and Technology Management. 2001

Tiratsoo N The "Americanization" of management education in Britain. Journal of Management Inquiry, 2004, Vol. 13, No. 2, pp. 118–126

Weller M, Dillon P Education and business partnerships in the United Kingdom: Initiatives in search of a rationale. Bulletin of Science, Technology and Society, 1999, Vol. 19, No. 1, pp. 60–67

Using Kolb's Learning Cycle to Teach Negotiation Skills

J. Rosiński* and J. Klich

Jagiellonian University, Kraków, Poland

Introduction

This chapter presents a case study of a module of a course within a tertiary education curriculum at the Institute of Economics and Management and is chosen to illustrate the way the learning cycle developed by Kolb is used to teach negotiation skills to entrepreneurs. The course is based on two assumptions:

1. Negotiation skills rely largely on (stable) personality traits (extroversion, flexibility, conciliatory manner).
2. Effectiveness of adult education depends on many aspects, e.g. on class structure as defined by Kolb (Rosiński and Rychlicka 2001). This is a widely recognized observation (see e.g. Senge et al. 2002).

Kolb's learning cycle model comprises four stages and the main thesis rests on the requirement that all four stages of the process must be completed for the process to be effective (see Fig. 1 on the next page). Many models of (academic) teaching focus on reflection leading to the formulation of a universal model; often ignoring the question of application of the uncovered rules, concentrating rather on explaining of the phenomena at hand and on predicting their future form. Traditional teaching validates less the contribution of the learners in the process of designating meaning, and does not recognize the need of using emotions in the process of (group) learning: it focuses on dissemination of specialist knowledge.

P.C. van der Sijde et al. (eds.), *Teaching Entrepreneurship.*
© Physica-Verlag Berlin Heidelberg 2008

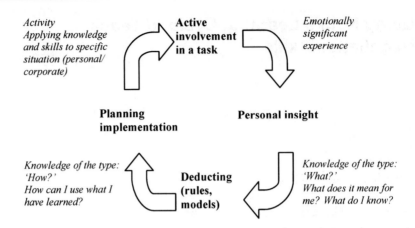

Fig. 1 Learning cycle of Kolb (Senge et al. 2002)

This learning model for entrepreneurship seems distinct from the model preferred in traditional learning (see Fig. 2: accommodator on the next page). An efficient entrepreneur is expected to display traits and skills typical of persons successfully holding sales-related positions (or in sales and marketing departments) and for those who function effectively in positions that require social dexterity (e.g. in public relations departments). This way of functioning is characteristic of the accommodator/hands-on type; this in contrast to assimilator type in traditional academic learning settings. In other words, by applying the traditional model we 'generate' successive assimilators in stead of accommodators; the dilemma of the entrepreneurship teacher. The dilemma might be resolved by incorporating the complete learning cycle Kolb into academic teaching.

Application of Kolb to Teaching Negotiation Skills

The above assumptions concerning the specifics of entrepreneurship and learner attitudes are given consideration in a 45-hr. social communication and negotiation course. The course is in workshop form and the classes are run in 6-hr. blocks. Besides fulfilling the above mentioned assumptions regarding teaching, it was crucial to adopt a methodology suitable to specific subject matter. As negotiation may be understood in a plethora of ways, a decision had to be made on one leading approach.

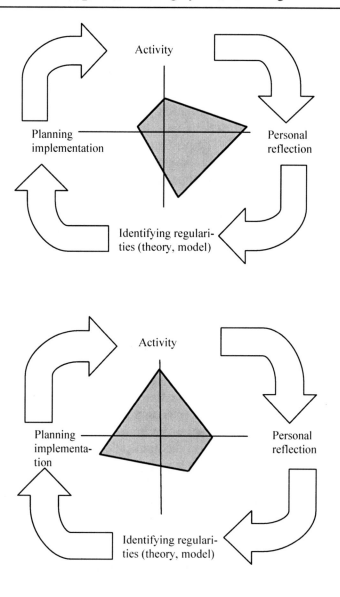

Fig. 2 Learning styles: Assimilator (*top*), Accommodator (*bottom*)

Four fundamental approaches to the issue of negotiation were distinguished (Mastenbroek 1996):

- Process with clearly distinct stages.
- As a set of guidelines and tactics.

- As persuasive communication.
- As the art of 'marrying' the opposites and resolving dilemmas.

The opening stage of the classes is built around the concept of negotiations as the art of marrying opposites. Such an approach reinforces the attitude of the person in the negotiation process. It also enables the introduction of core theoretical notions (e.g. negotiation style, attitude to the situation of negotiation, etc). The next step is that of negotiation as a process. This approach sees the negotiation as specific activities taking place in time and in a wider context (time, the sequence of events, and interdependence of actions). Only when the participants have reinforced their personal resources and once they understand the process, are they ready for information on persuasive negotiation and on the rules and tactics involved. Each session is thus constructed to include the Kolb learning cycle at least twice in a 6-hr. module. Every class starts with a game or case study or experiment, which allows a start of the cycle of adult learning (see Fig. 2) from the stage of Active Experimenting. The next stage (Reflective Observation) allows gathering reflections upon the negotiation game. Often this stage takes on a form of discussion between the persons in a group with the teacher, taking on the role of moderator in the discussion. The next stage is that of the conclusion of the discussion, conducted by the teacher (see Fig. 1). It is possible to make use of a presentation; however it is more useful to make a conceptualization of the material provided by the participants. The winding up stage (planning/implementation) may take the form of a moderated group discussion or brainstorming on the application or a short lecture of the trainer on the application of the knowledge. The choice of the form of closing the learning cycle depends largely on the experience of the group. Groups characterized by low experience (first year students) welcome ready ideas of knowledge implementation, whereas groups with more experience (students of final years of university have certain experience of working in various organizations of this type) have more positive reactions when invited to share their experience or use their experience to find applications for what they learned.

Construction of a Single Session of the Course

To exemplify this model we take one of the sessions early in the course. The classes concentrate on understanding negotiation as a way of combining opposites and resolving dilemmas. The learning cycle starts with the experiment of the type: Caring for your business based on Mastenbroek's model. The stages of learning relate to all four fundamental dimensions.

The exercises provide feedback on individual negotiation styles. As a result, not only do the participants' behaviours improve but participants also gain new knowledge. Table 1 gives more detailed information on this particular course.

Table 1 Structure of the negotiation workshop according to Kolb's learning cycle

Learning cycle stage 1			
Specific experience	*Reflective observation*	*Abstract generalization*	*Active experimentation*
Negotiation game Stock Edelweiss	Moderated discussion	Mastenbroek Model: elements of negotiator's behaviour that affect the 'Looking after business' dimension – a multimedia presentation	Real life examples of the behaviours increasing ' Looking after business'
Remarks			
Negotiation games were derived from the book by Mastenbroek (1996)			The trainer shapes the discussion by providing examples from his/her own life, and then invites the participants to follow suit. Providing 3–4 personal examples 'sparkles the fuse' and ignites in participants the willingness to share their own experience
Closing the D.A. Kolb cycle. Result: one of the negotiation's dimensions is grasped: 'Looking after business'. This understanding is combined with adequate courses of actions and backed up by experiences from the participants own lives.			
Learning cycle stage 2			
Specific experience	*Reflective observation*	*Abstract generalization*	*Active experimentation*
Negotiation game Sharks Island	Moderated discussion	Model of Mastenbroek: elements of negotiator's behaviour influencing the dimension: 'Building strength' – multimedia presentation	Real life examples of the behaviours increasing ' Building strength' dimension
Remarks			
Negotiation games were derived from the book by Mastenbroek (1996)			This element of the cycle does not require much time as the pattern of behaviour appeared in the earlier cycle of D.A. Kolb and by now the participants are well aware of the desirable behaviours
Winding up the D.A. Kolb cycle. Result: dimensions of 'Flexibility' and 'Atmosphere' are introduced, alongside the adequate course of action, additionally combined with participants' own experiences.			

Learning cycle stage 3			
Specific experience	*Reflective observation*	*Abstract generalization*	*Active experimentation*
Negotiation game The Eggs of Dodo Bird	Moderated discussion	Model of Mastenbroek: elements of negotiator's behaviour influencing the dimensions: 'Flexibility' and 'Atmosphere' – multimedia presentation	
Remarks			
Negotiation games were derived from the book by W. Mastenbroek (1996)			Examples taken from real life and from business

Winding up the D.A. Kolb cycle. Result: dimensions of 'Flexibility' and 'Atmosphere' are introduced, alongside the adequate course of action, in addition to the participants' own experiences.

Learning cycle stage 4			
Specific experience	*Reflective observation*	*Abstract generalization*	*Active experimentation*
Negotiation game	Small-group discussion of the game outcome	Presentation of the game results on the group forum	Conclusions regarding application of the desirable behaviours observed when playing the game
Remarks			
May concern any subject and scenario and should meet the following criteria: possible integration solution (satisfying interests of both parties involved), relatively broad extent of potential agreement, the scenario should contain 3–5 negotiation issues (e.g. item price, pay-by date, after-sales guarantees, timetable of deliveries). The game should be played in 4-person teams, where two persons are negotiating and two are observers	Discussion of the game in 4-person groups. The persons who were observers give feedback, by using the categories of the Mastenbroek model, i.e. 'Looking after Business', 'Building Strength', ' Atmosphere', 'Flexibility'	As the negotiation game provided a broad scope for integration agreement, it is possible to compose a ranking of the achieved results and to establish what types of behaviour (within the model) led to the advantageous solutions	Discussion concerns applications in subsequent negotiation groups, everyday life situations, business negotiations

Closing the D.A. Kolb cycle. Result: The participants of the classes receive feedback on their personal negotiation styles (in the categories of the Mastenbroek model) and how these affect the negotiations outcomes. The participants know what behaviours positively affect the outcomes of integrated negotiation.

Further Use of the Kolb Model

Undoubtedly, any application of the model in non-academic organizations may entail the necessity to change the proportions of the realization time: less time spent on the theoretical presentation at the simultaneous increase of time spent on presenting practical application. However it is the authors' opinion that it is more viable to adhere to the model presented in this chapter, as those in business organizations need reflection of a more universal character. This reflection enables them to find by themselves a wider range of application of knowledge and skills, whereas by providing them with long lists of ready-made solutions we may curtail their creativity. Naturally, in the learning process, the participants have to be presented with a certain number of possible applications and references to their life. However – metaphorically speaking – some leavening is needed for the participants to bake bread themselves. Presenting a long list of possible applications is like serving sliced bread in a packet. No one is interested in baking their own bread when a ready-made loaf is at hand.

References

Mastenbroek W (1996) Negotiations, PWN, Warsaw

Rosiński J, Rychlicka A (2001) "Stronę uczenia przez rozwiązywanie problemów" (Learning Through Problem Solving) in: Borkowski T [ed.] "Dylematy kształcenia menedżerów u progu XXI wieku" (Dilemmas of the Education of Managers at the turn of the XXIst century), Wydawnictwo Akademickie, Krakow

Senge PM, Kleiner A, Roberts CH, Ross RB, Smith BJ (2002) Piąta dyscyplina, materiały dla praktyka. Jak budować organizację uczącą się; (The Fifth Discipline. Practitioner manual. How to Build the Learning Organisation), Oficyna Ekonomiczna, Krakow

Entrepreneurial Learning and Virtual Learning Environment

P. Kyrö*, T. Kauppi, and M. Nurminen

University of Tampere, Tampere, Finland

Introduction

Both entrepreneurial and virtual learning are phenomena that have risen in the turn of the twenty-first century. The needs of the society as well as the technical innovations have sped up their development. The European Union has set entrepreneurial practices as one of the central goals in active citizenship (the European Commission 1999). Finland is committed to it throughout its education system (European Commission 2002). To reach this goal, the Ministry of Education has launched a policy programme for entrepreneurship education. The programme emphasises the importance of entrepreneurship education as a part of teachers basic and extension studies. (Opetusministeriö 2004). However, the educational research of the dynamics of entrepreneurial learning has hardly begun. Mainly, this discourse has taken place in business disciplines and in some extent in the field of technology. The American view of both entrepreneurship and education influences the dialogue (Kyrö 2005). The conceptualisation of education oriented discourse is still fragmented and searching for its forms. However, a new European multi-scientific wave is rising in the contemporary research and this study follows this tradition. It focuses on the cultural background, innovative processes and the dynamics of learning in entrepreneurship (for example Fayolle, Ulijn and Kyrö 2005). When it comes to the virtual learning Finland is among those in the forefront in its development. For example in educational sector it has a special strategy programme following mainstreaming principles and in universities we have own programme for national virtual university (Opetusministeriö 2000). Recently virtual learning researches have identified an increasing need to focus more on social, interactive and networking learning practises (Sallila and Kalli 2002). Internet-based

P.C. van der Sijde et al. (eds.), *Teaching Entrepreneurship.*
© Physica-Verlag Berlin Heidelberg 2008

learning environments offer one tool to meet this challenge. For example Hakkarainen (2002) regards them as the most promising new technology applications for that purpose. As an example he describes the Canada-based "Future Learning Environment (FLE)-project". Other examples of different projects that face these questions are, for instance, Finnish "The IQ Form" and "Metodix" that focuses on scientific research (Niemi and Ruohotie 2002, http://www.metodix.com). All three examples represent learning platforms that are rather widely used in respect to Finnish population. The latest statistics of Metodix reports that it has 3,900 registered users and 20,000 average visits/month.

Together entrepreneurial learning and a virtual learning environment offer an interesting, fast evolving combination that challenges us to explore and create new practices and solutions. At the same time, it challenges us to both consider the theoretical basis of a learning environment and to develop a practical platform. Following these challenges this article approaches the development of a virtual learning environment from the entrepreneurial learning perspective. First, it constructs a conceptual framework of entrepreneurship education. The framework locates the role of an entrepreneurial learner and learning in the field of entrepreneurship education. Then it defines the qualities of an entrepreneurial learner and learning. They determine the basis for building an entrepreneurial, learner centred virtual learning environment EntreNet. Finally, we describe how the Entre-Net meets the constructed pedagogical criteria of entrepreneurial learning.

The Conceptual Framework for Entrepreneurship Education

Identifying the elements of entrepreneurship education can be started by looking at the terms used for it. A study conducted in 1989 by the Durham University Business School identified differences between the USA, Canada, UK and other European countries. The term *entrepreneurship* education was familiar in the USA and Canada whereas the term *enterprise* education was used in the UK. In the UK, the focus was on an *entrepreneur*. Also, Erkkilä's dissertation "Entrepreneurial education" studying these concepts in the USA, UK and Finland, revealed differences in terms (Erkkilä 2000). In order to avoid conceptual confusion Erkkilä suggests that we should use a single concept of *"entrepreneurial education"*. Alain Gibb poses that there is a substantial synonymy between entrepreneurial and enterprising behaviour. The only major distinction that can be made is that an entrepreneur actor is traditionally associated with business activity (Gibb 1993). In his later writings Gibb (2001) used these terms as synonyms. Thus, in identifying the elements of this phenomenon, we have to lean mostly on Anglo-American terminology that focuses on the terms "entrepreneurship", "enterprise", "enterprising", "entrepreneurial" and "entrepreneur". Conceptually, it is easy to argue that these terms are not comparable, but rather focus on different elements of the phenomenon. Each of these poses a different question in education. The question who is supposed to learn gets the answer – an entrepreneur. What is the target of our learning gives us the terms "enterprise" or "entrepreneurship" and, finally, what kind of a learner or learning we refer to gives us the answer "enterprising" or "entrepreneurial." Consequently, in defining our concept we have to choose between two terms for our phenomenon and two terms for the qualities of that phenomenon. Thus, we ask the question: is our phenomenon an enterprise or entrepreneurship. In this respect, I believe there is a consensus that it is rather entrepreneurship than an enterprise (e.g. Gartner 1990). Thus, from the perspective of education these questions have actually identified the basic elements and phenomenon. This is shown in Fig. 1.

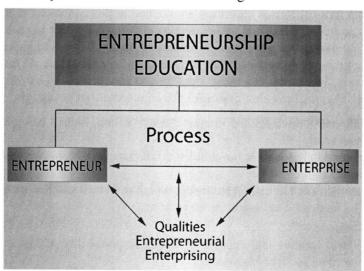

Fig. 1 The framework for the concept of entrepreneurship education

Therefore, it is possible to suggest that entrepreneurship education concerns entrepreneurs, entrepreneurial/enterprising processes and, as an outcome, the enterprise to whatever context or conceptual content it relates to, as well as the dynamics between them.

urial Learner and Learning

entrepreneurship, starting from its earliest definitions in the , relates to action and actors (Haahti 1989; Petrin 1991). In French entrepreneurship meant doing, going forward and taking initiative. In English it has meant an exiting and unknown experience as well as risk-taking in assignments. Only in the seventeenth century inspired by the Enlightenment the scientific basis for entrepreneurship started to develop. The transitional interpretation of the history of entrepreneurship reveals its purpose, qualities and forms, which profile an entrepreneurial learner and learning (Kyrö 2000, 2005).The early contributors of the Enlightenment described an entrepreneur as a unique and free individual, who had ability, will and right to create his/her own place in the society. This entrepreneur created a new kind of welfare in a society by recognizing opportunities and exploiting them by combining resources in a new way and applying new knowledge. The entrepreneur and entrepreneurship opposed and broke the hereditary system, privileges and institutions, such as the feudal system, guild system and mercantilism as well as created new models for action. Also the roots of formal education are planted in this contexts and its idea of human being. Education and entrepreneurship were closer to each other then than during our generation. The idea of human being was based on a holistic relationship between man and nature, where the nature set the rules for living. We can employ these ideas also to entrepreneurial learning and learner. Thus we have four principles for entrepreneurial pedagogy:

1. Life and knowledge are created through action, human being/learner is an actor.
2. Human being/learner has a holistic relationship with his/her environment.
3. Learner has a holistic relationship with him/herself and his/her action.
4. The human being/learner as an actor is:

   – unique
   – free, creative and capable of taking responsibility of his/her own actions and its consequences.

The bond between the individual and collective practices was lost in the modern era when the separate fields of science developed and the role of human action disappeared from the economics and organizational theories. Entrepreneurship research focused on the problems of small businesses, especially to the genetic traits of an entrepreneur. Only in the twenty-first century it expanded to the research on entrepreneurial processes and the most recent studies has again found the bond between individual and collective practices (Timmons 1994; Eijnatten 2005; Fayolle et al. 2005). Therefore, when it comes to entrepreneurship education on the one hand we can rely on the early contributors, on the other search for solutions from the latest research. For example Alan Gibb's (1993, 2001) research in the 1990s on entrepreneurial behaviour follows the original meaning of entrepreneurship. According to Gibb, entrepreneurial behaviour involves seeking opportunities and grabbing them, taking initiative and creating action, creative problem solution, autonomic leadership, taking the responsibility, ability to see things through, effective networking to control interaction, combining things creatively, assessing things and taking calculated risks. Principles for entrepreneurial virtual learning and a learning environment involve both a combination of these qualities and most recent studies on virtual learning.

Basis for Entrepreneurial Virtual Learning Environment

A unique individual's free, holistic and collaborative action is the basis for building a learning environment. Thus it relates to the behaviour of a learner in an environment, his/her competences to recognize and exploit opportunities as well as to collaborate with co' learners. Our aim has been to expand the current understanding of virtual reality. From a computer-generated simulation of the real world as Oxford English Dictionary defined it in 1992, we rather return to the broader definitions of virtuality as a supposed, possibly existing, yet unreal and imagined, but still "acting as such though not so called or defined", "being in practice though not in strictly or in name" as Penguin (Garmonsway and Simpson 1975) and Oxford (Thompson et al. 1992) dictionaries defined it. Employing these definitions requires combining them to real practices, since the action in entrepreneurial learning is real, not simulated and it also generates new real action. In other words, a learner creates a new reality virtually with other actors. Thus a virtual environment offers an asyncronic arena for learners and their collaboration. This is a challenge identified in latest research of learning environments. For example Hakkarainen's (2002) evaluation of the challenges and opportunities in online learning stresses the learner's possibility to build his/her own reality and learning environment instead of using ready-made decision paths and action models. Additionally, he speaks for interaction between other learners and their communities. The problem is that virtual learning is still seen as technical information-oriented, cognitive activity rather than learners own, concrete action (e.g. Griffiths 1999; Leiner et al. 1999). The action-based entrepreneurial learning differs from the cognitive view and thus challenges the cognitive learning paradigm. Comparing to the constructivism, it also has a stronger focus on action and creativeness, though alongside with inner thought and past experiences.

The concept of a free actor and the definition of autonomy get new characteristics in virtual learning. Kiviniemi (2002) sees it as controlling personal learning and describes autonomy as a situation where the student takes responsibility of his/her studies and develops a critical view towards learning contents. In entrepreneurial learning the possibility of obtaining information freely from the surrounding reality and its actors is a central part of freedom. In addition, it includes the freedom to form interactive societies and acquire the needed resources. Uniqueness combined with freedom means that we take different learners and their backgrounds equally into account. That is a real challenge for developing virtual learning environments. It does not only mean that the environment itself offers different material for different learners, but it has to be equally accessible and take cultural differences into account. For instance, at a moment virtual learning is mainly the privilege of rich countries. One fifth of all countries possess 90% of Internet connections (UNDP 1999). On the other hand, research shows differences in Internet use between men and women as well as between young and old. In 1997 15% of the users were women and most of all users were relatively young (Järvinen 1997). And for example women are more interested in WWW-pages and discussion forums, whereas the men in games and news (Suomen Gallup 1999). This means that it is important to consider different interests, learning styles and cultures in developing virtual learning. In order to consider all these aspect we employed and modified Nonaka's and his colleagues' dynamic knowledge creation model.

The Dynamic Knowledge Creation Model for EntreNet

According to Nonaka et al. (2002) knowledge creation is both a continuous and self-transcending process, created in interactions amongst individuals or between individuals and their environment. Nonaka et al. divide knowledge in two types: explicit and tacit knowledge. Explicit knowledge can be expressed in a formal and systematic way but tacit knowledge is difficult to formalize and communicate to others. It is subjective insights, intuitions, mental models and mutual trust and it is rooted in action, procedures, values and emotions (Nonaka et al. 2002). They propose a dynamic knowledge creation model which consists of three elements that interact with each other (Fig. 2):

1. The SECI process where knowledge is created in interaction between tacit and explicit knowledge
2. The shared context for knowledge creation
3. Knowledge assets; the inputs, outputs and moderator of the knowledge creating process

The SECI process has influenced to the formation of EntreNet learning environment by being one of the theoretical bases of its creation.

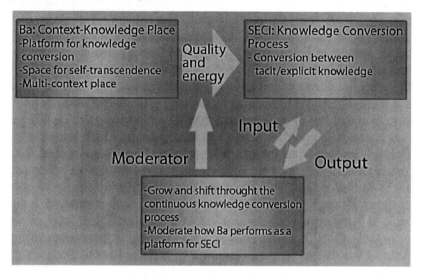

Fig. 2 Three elements of the knowledge creating process

The SECI process consists of four modes of knowledge conversation:

1. Socialization (tacit->tacit)
2. Externalization (tacit->explicit)
3. Combination (explicit->explicit)
4. Internalization (explicit->tacit)

By knowledge creation Nonaka et al. (2002) mean interaction between tacit and explicit knowledge. "Socialization is the process of converting new tacit knowledge through shared experiences". Tacit knowledge is difficult to formalize so it can be acquired only through shared experience, such as spending time together or having social meetings. Socialization applies to learning through hands-on experience, rather than reading manuals or textbooks. This is a real challenge for virtual environment – how to enhance real experience change and sharing. This is why we put much effort to enhance collaboration in EntreNet. Externalization means the process where tacit knowledge is converted into explicit knowledge. Knowledge is crystallised when tacit knowledge is articulated into explicit one. When knowledge can be shared with others it can form a basis for new knowledge. The strong advantage of virtual collaborative learning is that participants have to explicate their intentions and ideas in a written form. Combination converts explicit knowledge into more complex and systematic sets of explicit knowledge. In this process explicit knowledge is collected and then combined to form new knowledge. Knowledge can be synthesized from many different sources. The asyncronic qualities of virtual learning enhance the possibilities to gather knowledge and experiences from all around and then return to the environment and share them with others when and where ever it is convenient for the learner. Internalization is the process where explicit knowledge is embodied into tacit knowledge and it is closely related to learning by doing. Textbook and manuals provide information that has to be actualised through action and practice. Internalization converts explicit knowledge in textbooks into tacit knowledge by individuals and enriches their tacit knowledge base (Nonaka et al. 2002). In entrepreneurial learning we also regard communication as action and it leads to further action. This is one of the leading principles in EntreNet. Movement through the SECI-process forms a spiral instead of a circle (Fig. 3). It is a dynamic process that starts from the individual level, expands over organisational boundaries as it moves through communities of interaction and thus knowledge creation never ends (Nonaka et al. 2002). Virtual communication in EntreNet offers an excellent arena for crossing these boundaries.

Knowledge needs a context to be created. Ba offers such a context. It is a Japanese term for "place". Here it is defined as a shared context in which knowledge is shared, created and utilised. Ba is the place where information is interpreted to become knowledge. It focuses on interaction, where knowledge is created together with other people, not individually. The participants in ba cannot be mere onlookers; they have to take part in the activities. This is also the case with EntreNet, where everyone is encouraged into action in many different ways. The environment itself promotes the student's autonomy and independent action. In group environment the teacher has little control over the functionalities. The students form groups themselves and are able to decide on accepting new members, assigning user rights to others and forming new groups. The teacher provides the place and time, ba, for the students, who themselves then act in the environment. Like ba, the group environment is empty without participants. The content is created by groups and group members, without them, the environment loses its purpose

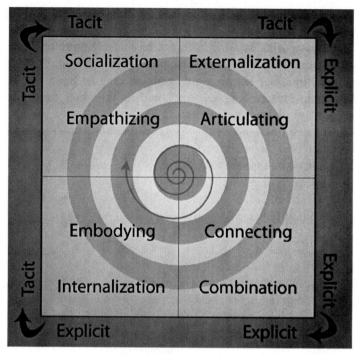

Fig. 3 The SECI process

(Nonaka et al. 2002). There are four types of ba, originating, dialoguing, systemizing and exercising ba. They are defined by two dimensions of interactions (Fig. 4, next page). One dimension is the type of interaction, which can be individual or collective. The other one is the media of the interaction, face-to-face or virtual. Virtual media can be anything from books to teleconferences (Nonaka et al. 2002). *Originating* ba is individual face-to-face interaction. It is the only way to capture all the physical senses and psycho-emotional reactions such as ease or discomfort, which are important in sharing tacit knowledge. *Dialoguing* ba is defined by collective and face-to-face interactions. It is where the individuals' mental models and skills are shared, converted into common terms and articulated as concepts. It offers a context for externalisation, where the individuals' tacit knowledge is shared and articulated amongst participants. *Systemizing* ba is collective and virtual interaction. It offers a context for combination of existing explicit knowledge, which can easily be transmitted to a large number of people in written form. *Systemizing* ba includes group information systems such as group e-mails and news groups. Exercising ba is defined by individual and virtual interactions. It offers a context for internalisation, where individuals embody explicit knowledge that is communicated through virtual media. Exercising ba synthesizes the transcendence and reflection through action (Nonaka et al. 2002). This model together with the principles of entrepreneurial learning offers a basis for EntreNet. However, it also contains complex problems that need to be solved. Next, we will describe how EntreNet learning environment on one hand has benefited from Nonaka and his colleagues' work and on the other hand pursued to solve the problems it brings along.

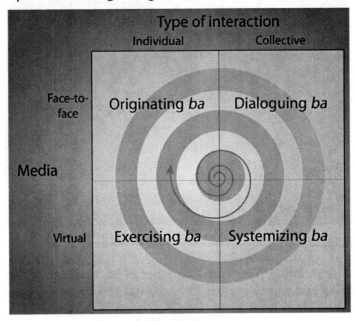

Fig. 4 Four types of ba

EntreNet Learning Environment Concept

EntreNet is a third generation learning environment. It is an international environment meant for science-based entrepreneurship learning and research. The first phase of the environment was launched in 1997 when Metodix environment, which was devoted to scientific and applied research and methods, was created by multi-scientific expert group (Linturi 1998). Its second generation phase, expanded to enhance virtual interaction and to develop tools for conducting research and creating content. The aim was to create a meeting place for researchers, method developers, research students and teachers where they could interact with each other regardless of place and time. As a learning environment it supports self guided and social learning, which is based on problem solving. The users can apply methodological knowledge by using method tools. (http://www.metodix.com). EntreNet concept takes advantage of these experiences, but also aims to be more holistic, collaborative and strongly dependent on context.

Holistic Approach to Action

The environment as a whole, but also its sub-environments, form a holistic, action-based entity. As a basis, the learner comes to the environment and each of its sub-environments in order to do specific tasks related to learning and researching entrepreneurship education. The tools are selected from the actor's, not the technique's, point of view. On the other hand, the sub-environments form a network of functions that serves different dimensions of learning and cooperation. EntreNet learning environment offers a ba for students. Interaction takes place through a virtual media and the type of interaction can be both individual and collective. However we would like to represent the idea of not making such a boundary between these media because action is more important in entrepreneurial learning than the media that is used. The media just offer different kinds of tools that concentrate on the main focus, learning and creating knowledge through action. EntreNet is built to support entrepreneurial learning and the main focus of entrepreneurial learning is action. EntreNet as a whole and its sub-environments form an action-based entity. Another main point for entrepreneurial learning is that a learner has a holistic relationship with him/herself and his/her actions. As Nonaka et al. (2002) say, ba offers a context for knowledge creation. EntreNet learning environment can offer holistic context for learners and their action because EntreNet is an action-based virtual environment that offers learners a chance to share experiences and work together for mutual goal. All the users of EntreNet share a common interest in and scientific orientation to entrepreneurship education. The concept of group forming brings about autonomy on the individual's and society's level. It makes cooperative learning possible as a natural part of learning.

The needs of different learners have been taken into account in the sub-environments based on the purpose of action. All of them have the same navigational elements that make intuitive navigation and learning possible regardless of the learners' skills. The ease of navigation and usability are improved with graphics. The graphics are designed using a pedagogical approach. The pictures should be informative and offer something extra to the user. The navigational pictures on the opening pages of all sub-environments function as maps showing the user all available activities. These also aim to create curiosity and support creativity regardless of the learner's cultural background with symbolism, form and colour. The aim of the graphics in the environment is to form a welcoming and friendly atmosphere. The graphics of the EntreNet (Fig. 5) try to make users forget that they are in a technical surroundings so that it will be easier to concentrate on the contents of the learning environment instead of its' technology. Their aim is, also, to raise the users' interests by an artistic, soft appearance and symbolism. The theme, space, was originally chosen because of its richness in symbolism and metaphor. All the sub-environments are planets, with distinctive looks and colours. The planets were assigned to sub-environments according to their symbolism and its correspondence to the content. The interface is designed to be easy to use. The index-page shows all the sub-environments, or planets, and a few of the basis functions such as news and discussion forum. When the user proceeds to an opening page of any sub-environment, a navigational picture will appear. The picture represents all the actions that are possible in that sub-environment. For example, in group environment, the opening page informs the user that he/she is able to work in the groups, join and leave groups as well as create new ones. Inside the environment all the other planets are available on the top of the page. The sub-environment-specific functions are shown in the left margin. These navigational structures will remain the same in all sub-environments making the environment logical and easy to navigate. The actors may have different roles in the environment. They can be the users or producers of material, learners, co-learners, teachers or administrators according to the situation and their own needs. The first sub-environment, *entrepreneurship research*, consists of previous research, "what has been researched before". The users will find scientific entrepreneurship education material that fulfils the criteria of scientific research.

The material helps the learner to, consciously or unconsciously, form an opinion on the criteria of scientific entrepreneurship research. It is also a faster way to get a hold of new research results compared to the traditional printed publications. Another sub-environment, *methods,* consists of method articles, "how the research has been conducted". The articles, or manuscripts, can include sound, pictures, animation and video in addition to text. Thus the sub-environment supports pedagogical diversity. Through these two sub-environments the learners are able to, in an entrepreneurial manner, use the available information and combine it freely. Because of the versatile

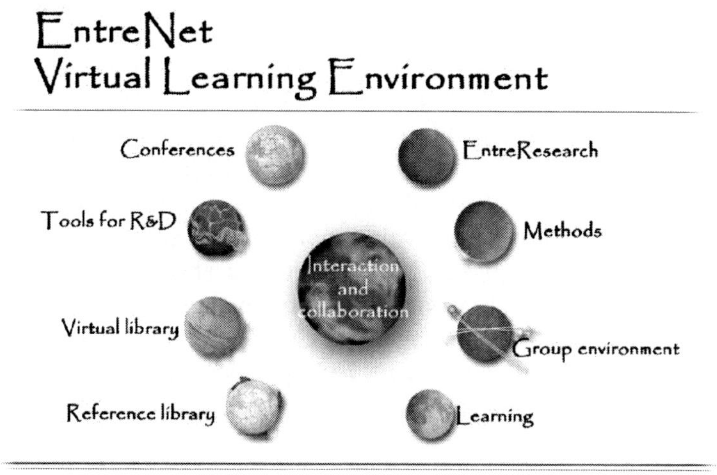

EntreNet
Virtual Learning Environment

Conferences

EntreResearch

Tools for R&D

Methods

Interaction and collaboration

Virtual library

Group environment

Reference library

Learning

Fig. 5 Front page and structure of EntreNet

articles and manuscripts the learners are able to find new possibilities and ways for action, as well as take a critical view on learning contents. The next sub-environment, *group environment*, enables the students to form groups independently. In addition, the discussion forum and group e-mail makes interaction possible between learners. Group members can save documents and read each other's work in the file area. The students can form networks and interact with each other spontaneously and freely based on their own needs and interests. The students can initiate the formation of new groups. The group environment enables networking, team forming and collaboration between learners. *Interactive learning environment* differs from the group environment in that the teacher has the initiative there. The environment is meant for taking courses; it includes a calendar, a file area and a possibility to take notes. It is similar to other learning platforms available, but it is meant to increase the autonomy of the teacher. In the interactive learning environment teachers can plan and organize learning, however, the responsibility of the actual learning is still on student's shoulders. The next sub-environments are *reference library* and *virtual library*. The reference library offers information on the available material both in the environment and in other databases. The student can, for instance, fetch an available book from a library. The virtual library consists of direct links to material available in databases. The student is able to read the material online or print it. The libraries help in finding, obtaining and using resources. Automated robots make sure the links are always working. *Research and development tools* are the seventh sub-environment.

There the students are able to use virtual research tools in order to conduct their own research thus learning by doing and at the same time creating new knowledge for themselves, for co-learners and for the scientific community. The eighth sub-environment, *conferences*, is aimed for arranging conferences, thus it is also focused on action. It enables participants to have their research results reflected widely and form research networks. Conference managers will find the environment useful for arranging conferences. The activities begin with announcement and marketing of the event and participant registering. After that the abstracts and papers are saved to the file area and evaluated and commented after which they are published. The conference manager can choose the functionalities needed for a conference. Not all conferences have identical profile and include the same functions. For instance, it is possible to choose whether the evaluation process is a blind evaluation or not and whether all participants have access to the file area to read abstracts and give their comments. We aim to arrange virtual conferences in the environment.

Dynamic Knowledge Creation in EntreNet

Socialization: Group environment is open for both formal and informal groups. There users can share thoughts and learn to trust each other because they can freely form new groups. Users also learn to work with each other and this encourages the spreading of tacit knowledge. Knowledge outside of the entrepreneurship education field enriches the knowledge base (wandering outside). This occurs, for example, when students of different occupational backgrounds bring their insights into the learning situation. Socialization happens also in a knowledge exchange between research in the field (wandering inside). R&D tools provide learning through hands-on-experience. *Externalization*: The need to work in the groups and do team work forces users to try to articulate their tacit knowledge in an explicit way. The tacit knowledge of an individual becomes common knowledge, written in an essay or report and is thus converted into explicit knowledge. In addition, in the discussion forum the learners are encouraged to share their views with each other. In virtual environments this can be even stronger than in real life because people need to say everything in words and they cannot use for example gestures. Externalization can occur in interview assignments, where the tacit knowledge of the interviewee is converted into explicit knowledge in the students' final essay on the interview. *Combination*: The libraries, methods and research environments are open for users to collect and combine explicit data. The R&D environment also offers tools to combine collected explicit data. The data can be used in a new, context-specific combination. Especially in the conference environment the users are very close to new knowledge. *Internalization*: The conference-environment and the learning environment can be used to disseminate collected and combined data to students and researchers. so that they can use and adopt the knowledge. In EntreNet the discussion forums work as dialoguing ba, where the students can discuss and transform their tacit knowledge into explicit. EntreNet enables group e-mails for group's members. The discussion forum can act as a Systemizing ba; Method and research environments in EntreNet also work as mediums for information. Individual students can read articles and apply the knowledge in their own work. These elements form the exercising ba of the EntreNet. Originating ba is problematic in virtual learning environment since it doesn't allow participants to percept co-learners' immediate reactions and emotions. It is possible to some extent, when cameras and voice are integrated parts of computers.

Conclusions

EntreNet as a third generation virtual environment, we hope, will offer an attractive collaborative arena for researchers, students and teachers in the future. Together the sub-environments are individual and collective in that they take into account the differences in learners, other actors and groups. It is functionally flexible and provides the necessary functionalities and information to the user regardless of time and place. The content, structure and functionalities support opportunity recognition and exploitation thus by combining opportunities in a new way we hope to offer exiting experiences for future scientists. Thus as a whole the environment supports the production of a new reality virtually. Instead of knowing the learners produce, in an entrepreneurial way, the conditions of their own reality, take the risks involved and enjoy the fruits of their work.

References

Davidsson P, Delmar F and Wiklund J (2002) Entrepreneurship as growth: growth as entrepreneurship. In Hilt M and Ireland D (eds.) Strategic Entrepreneurship: Creating a New Mindset (pp. 328–342). Oxford: Blackwell

Eijnatten van FM (2005) A chaordic lens for understanding entrepreneurship and intrapreneurship. In Fayolle A, Kyrö P and Ulijn J (eds.) Entrepreneurship Research in Europe: Perspectives and Outcomes. Cheltenham: Edward Elgar

Erkkilä K (2000) Entrepreneurial Education. New York: Carland

European Commission (1999) Innovation in Europe – The Green Paper. Luxemburg: Jean Monnet Building

European Commision (2002) Final Report of the expert group "best procedure" project on education and training for entrepreneurship. November 2002

Fayolle A, Ulijn J and Kyrö P (eds) (2005) Entrepreneurship Research in Europe: Perspectives and Outcomes. Cheltenham: Edward Elgar

Garmonsway and Simpson (1975) English Dictionary. New York: Penguin

Gartner WB (1990) What are we talking about when we talk about entrepreneurship? Journal of Business Venturing, 5, 15–28

Gibb A (1993) The enterprise culture and education. Understanding enterprise education and its links with small business, entreprenurship and wider educational goals. International Small Business Journal 11/3, s. 11–24

Gibb A (2001) Creating conducive environments for learning and entrepreneurship. Living with, dealing with, creating and enjoying uncertainty and complexity. The First Conference of the Entrepreneurship Forum Entrepreneurship and Learning. Naples June 21–24 2001

Gibb A (2002) In pursuit of a new 'enterprise' and 'entrepreneurship' paradigm for learning. The International Journal of Management Reviews, Autumn 2002

Griffiths RT (1999) Internet for Historians, History of the Internet. The development of the Internet http://www.let.leidenuniv.nl/history/ivh/frame_theorie.html, Last Updated: 3-9-1999

Haahti AJ (1989) Entrepreneurs' strategic orientation. Modelling Strategic Behaviour In Small Industrial Owner-managed firms. The Helsinki School of Economics and Business Administration, Helsinki. Acta Academiae Oeconomicae Helsingiensis. Series A: 64

Hakkarainen K (2002) Aikuisen oppiminen verkossa. In Sallila P, Kalli P (eds.) "Verkot ja teknologia aikuisopiskelun tukena" s. 16–52. Aikuiskasvatuksen 42. vuosikirja. Kansanvalistusseura ja Aikuiskasvatuksen Tutkimusseura

Järvinen P (1997) Internet käyttäjäselvitys 1997. http://www.pjoy.fi./ tutkimus/ kt97/johdanto.htm 13.12.1997

Kiviniemi K (2002) Autonomian ja ohjauksen suhde verkko-opetuksessa. Aikuiskasvatuksen 42. vuosikirja. Kansanvalistusseura ja Aikuiskasvatuksen Tutkimusseura

Kyrö P (2000) Entrepreneurship in the Postmodern Society. Wirtschafts PolitischeBlätter 2000/47 Jahrgang/(ed.) Wien: Wirtschaftskammer Österreich, 2000. pp. 37–45

Kyrö P (2005). Introduction. In Fayolle A, Kyrö P and Uljin J. (eds.) Entrepreneurship Research in Europe: Perspectives and Outcomes. Cheltenham: Edward Elgar

Leiner BM, Cerf VG, Clark D, Kahn RE, Kleinrock L, Lynch DC, Postel J, Roberts LG and Wolff S (1999) A Brief History of the Internet. http://www.isoc.org/ internet/history/brief.html. 28.12.1999

Linturi H (1998) Tietoa läskillä ja ilman. Murros ja oppimisympäristö. Aikuiskasvatus 1/98 s. 33–48

Niemi H and Ruohotie P (eds) (2002) Theoretical Understandings for Learning in the Virtual University. Tampereen yliopisto

Opetusministeriö (2000) Koulutuksen ja tutkimuksen tietostrategia 2000–2004

Petrin T (1991) Entrepreneurship and its development in public enterprises. In Prokopenko J and Pavlin (eds.) Entrepreneurship Development in Public Enterprises, I. International Labour Office Geneva. Management Development Series No. 29 p. 15–20. International Centre for Public Enterprises in Developing Countries, Ljubljana

Sallila P and Kalli P (eds) (2002) "Verkot ja teknologia aikuisopiskelun tukena" Aikuiskasvatuksen 42. vuosikirja. Kansanvalistusseura ja Aikuiskasvatuksen Tutkimusseura

Suomen Gallup (1999) http://www.gallubweb.com, 24.12.1999

Timmons J (1994) New Venture Creation. Entrepreneurship for the 21st Century. 4th edition. Illinois: Irwin

Thompson D et al (eds) (1992) Oxford English Dictionary. Oxford: Oxford University Press

UNDP (1999) Human Development Report. New York: Oxford Unversity Press

Nonaka I, Toyama R and Konno N (2002) SECI, Ba and leadership: a unified model of dynamic knowledge creation. In Little S, Quintas P and Ray T Managing knowledge, An Essential Reader (pp. 41–67). London: Sage Publications

Lightning Source UK Ltd.
Milton Keynes UK
UKOW030939020312

188144UK00004B/4/P